TEACHING THE SKILLS OF CONFLICT RESOLUTION

Activities and Strategies for Counselors and Teachers

David Cowan • Susanna Palomares • Dianne Schilling

cover design by Doug Armstrong Graphic Design
illustrations by Roger Johnson

ISBN 1-56499-008-7

For information about Teaching the Skills of Conflict Resolution Training Workshops and other materials, please write or call:

INNERCHOICE PUBLISHING
P.O. Box 1185, Torrance, CA 90505
Tel.:   (310) 816-3085
Fax: (310) 816-3092
E-Mail: blwjalmar@worldnet.att.net

TEACHING THE SKILLS OF CONFLICT RESOLUTION

Jalmar Press and Innerchoice Publishing are happy to announce

a collaborative effort under which all Innerchoice titles will now be distributed

only through Jalmar Press.

To request the latest catalog of our joint resources for use by teachers, counselors

and other care-givers to empower children to develop inner-directed living and

learning skills

call us at: (800) 662-9662

or fax us at: (310) 816-3092

or send us a card at: P.O. Box 1185, Torrance, CA 90505

We're eager to serve you and the students you work with.

By the way, Jalmar Press has several new titles coming up that can give you all
the necessary tools to teach conflict resolution to all your students. One of the
new products is called
THE PEACEFUL CLASSROOM IN ACTION, by Naomi Drew
It shows how Learning the Skills of Peacemaking, Naomi's first book, has
effectively been used in the classroom over the past 11 years. It is aimed at
grades K - 6.

A second title is
NONVIOLENT COMMUNICATION: A Language of Compassion by
Dr. Marshall B. Rosenberg
The dynamic communication techniques that Dr. Rosenberg has developed
transform potential conflicts into peaceful dialogues. Outstanding simple tools to
defuse arguments. Applicable K - Adult.

Write or call for the latest information or to place your order.

Contents

HOW TO USE THIS BOOK

TEACHING THE SKILLS OF CONFLICT RESOLUTION is a developmental and sequential program of activities designed to 1) build a base of awareness, understanding, and skills required for conflict prevention and resolution, 2) give students practice using a variety of strategies for managing and resolving conflict, 3) create opportunities for students to apply those strategies to real-life problems and conflicts, and 4) encourage students to transfer their learning to the resolution of issues and conflicts in the family, community, nation, and world.

In order for the activities to have the impact intended, we strongly urge you to present the units in the order given. For example, implementing a negotiation or problem-solving activity (from the unit on strategies) before the students have been introduced to active listening (in the communications unit) will produce less than optimal results. You don't have to implement every activity in each unit, but do provide a sufficient number of experiences to ensure that the skills and concepts being taught receive plenty of practice and reinforcement.

We encourage you to adjust and modify activities to suit the ages, ability levels, cultural/ethnic backgrounds, and interests of your students. You will know best how to maximize the appropriateness and impact of each activity, so please take

those liberties. For example, if the instructions call for the students to write a story, and you work with children who are not yet writing on their own, you may choose to have them draw pictures instead—or you may elect to create a group story (Big Book) from the ideas they dictate to you.

Sharing Circles are a very important part of each unit in this book. The learning and insights derived from regular participation in Sharing Circles is central to the success of the program. Only two Sharing Circles are fully elaborated in each unit; however, we recommend that you select several additional topics from the list at the end of each unit. One cautionary note: If you have never facilitated a Sharing Circle, please take the time to read the introductory sections of this book that pertain to this unique process.

We applaud collaborative efforts between teachers and counselors, particularly in the area of conflict resolution. What a natural! So, if you are a counselor working with teachers in the classroom (or a teacher interested in asking a counselor to participate in your efforts), here is one way to share responsibilities while taking full advantage of each person's area of expertise: Have the teacher lead individual and group activities and the counselor facilitate sharing circles. If you try this, we'd love to hear about your experience. Please write or give us a call.

Introduction and Theory

When we hear the word conflict, most of us respond by thinking of something negative. The words the dictionary chooses to define conflict tend to support this inclination; words like *carnage, destruction, battle, warfare, fight,* and so on. Why is it that we rarely associate conflict with positive words and images? For example, when we're able to reach a compromise between two conflicting ideas we call that an *agreement.* Maybe conflict can be seen as an *opportunity for agreement.* Now that's something positive!

When we start thinking about conflict as *opportunity,* we soon begin to see that all the negative connotations we've associated with conflict in the past are really the outcomes of *unresolved* conflict. Conflict by itself is neither good nor bad, it just is. However, when conflict goes unmanaged and unresolved, it can turn into some pretty ugly things, as the dictionary attests.

Thinking about conflict as opportunity, and understanding that unresolved conflict can lead to negative and destructive outcomes, opens the doors to a whole new way of looking at and learning from conflict.

There are few things that we can say for sure, but one of them is that all of us will experience conflict in our lives from time to time. It's part of living in a world with other people. In fact, we would encounter conflict even if we were the only person alive on the planet, because we not only have conflict with others, we have conflict with ourselves. Think of a time when you had to make a tough decision. Part of you said, "yes" and another part said, "no." You were in conflict. In fact, it could be argued that conflict begins even before we are born (does the unborn really want to leave the womb?) and continues until we take our last breath, reluctantly yet resignedly letting go of life.

In *Teaching the Skills of Conflict Resolution,* we focus on conflict as an opportunity for growth and understanding, and look at the outcomes of unresolved conflict the way a cooking instructor might point out the consequences of waiting too long to take an upside-down cake out of the pan. We approach conflict not as an enemy to be feared, but as a reality of life to be understood. Because conflict is such a natural part of our lives, we'd prefer that children see it not as a conclusive event, whether positive *or* negative, but as an intermediary event that can lead to positive or negative results. We want children to think of every conflict as having within it the seeds of a positive outcome, while understanding that unmanaged, unresolved conflict can instead produce negative and sometimes destructive results.

We also want children to understand that effectively resolving a conflict doesn't necessarily eliminate the source of the conflict. In all likelihood, people will continue to hold divergent positions and opinions. However, when a conflict is well managed, it is possible for individuals to maintain their beliefs and at the same time understand, accommodate, and accept the beliefs of others.

The Dynamics of Conflict

Most people think of conflict as an event or condition involving more than one person. But whether conflict involves other people or is an inner struggle to reach a decision or resolve an issue, conflict begins in the mind. In the past few years we've learned much about the way the mind functions. From the cognitive neurosciences, we have begun to see the connections between our perceptions and responses to what goes on around us.

Mindworks

Everything we experience with our senses enters first into our subconscious mind, where it is interpreted and given value and priority. Based on this interpretation, chemical and electrical signals are transmitted throughout the body, triggering physical and emotional responses. At the same time, signals are sent to the conscious mind so that we can begin to *think about* the experience.

This flow of stimuli and information explains many of the things that we commonly experience in our lives, but so often take for granted; for example, all the activities we engage in without thinking—like walking and breathing. Walking begins with a decision at the conscious level, but once the decision has been made, walking is turned over to the subconscious, leaving the conscious mind free to think about destination, route, etc. Breathing, on the other hand, requires no conscious effort to begin. We can elect to consciously control our breathing, but can return that control to the subconscious at any time.

Two things determine how the subconscious interprets, gives value, assigns priority, and responds to what the senses tell it about the events going on in the environment. The first is called *genetic imprinting*. Inherited fears are examples of genetic imprints. For example, all of us are born with a fear of loud noises—this genetic imprint starts governing our behavior from birth.

The second and predominant source from which the subconscious receives data is our accumulated life experience—everything that we have *learned*. We respond to most events in our lives the way we've learned to respond by having had similar experiences in the past. The first time you burned a finger in an open flame, you experienced pain in association with bringing your finger in contact with the flame. Ever since that first experience, when in close proximity to an open fire you've responded with caution. You don't even have to think about it. If your finger accidentally touches the flame, you pull it back so quickly that you avoid any burn at all. You remove your finger from the flame not because you think about it at the conscious level, but because your senses feed the necessary information to the subconscious and you react *without* thinking. This type of patterned response is called a *habit*.

From Perceptions to Conflict

This stored body of information that has such a great influence on our behavior is called a *belief system*. A belief system is comprised of what we have come to believe about everything in our environment, both good and bad, true and false. Our beliefs about anything determine our behavior toward it. Our belief systems start developing as soon as we start becoming aware of things going on around us in infancy.

When everything in our environment is in harmony with our belief system, we experience a sense of comfort and well being. This is because our belief system defines our *comfort zone*. However, when something enters our environment that is not defined by our belief system (something new) or that challenges or contradicts one or more of our beliefs, we experience stress at the limits of our comfort zone. All of our wants and needs, likes and dislikes, hopes and fears are defined by our belief system. When our beliefs are challenged, we are in conflict and our first conscious perception is stress.

The comfort zone of every individual is defined by a different set of beliefs. Picture yourself going through life matching and mismatching your comfort zone with the comfort zones of other people, and you will understand why you experience conflict (no matter how insignificant) with something or someone almost every day. Small, seemingly inconsequential disagreements or misunderstandings are at the very bottom of the conflict scale, but they can grow far worse if left unresolved. Moreover, if we repeatedly fail to handle petty disagreements effectively, we reinforce bad conflict-resolution habits. Most people don't have to look far in their lives to find examples of little irritations that turned into intense struggles because they weren't given the right kind of attention.

Whether small or large, conflict occurs when we perceive our environment being out of harmony with our belief system. It is the process by which we attempt to restore that harmony that determines the quality of the outcomes we achieve. The habits we have formed and the skills we have acquired directly determine the results we produce any time we engage in conflict. Most of the time, these results are negative and that is why we have come to believe that conflict itself is negative. It is not. Conflict is a necessary part of living and when engaged in with skill almost always produces positive and satisfying results for everyone involved.

For most people, children included, conflict is an unsettling experience that begins with a feeling of confusion or loss of control. Most of us, in reacting to and dealing with conflict, have developed some very bad habits. As our discussion continues, keep in mind the important role the belief system plays in fostering habitual responses to situations where beliefs are challenged. This awareness will be of assistance as we begin to learn new ways of managing conflict.

Internal and External Conflict

We experience two kinds of conflict. External conflicts are those that involve two or more people. Internal conflicts occur within a single individual when conflicting beliefs and desires clash, often during times of decision making. Because we experience both internal and external conflict, we must develop the skills necessary to deal effectively with both.

How Conflicts Get Started

Every conflict begins with someone or something intruding our comfort zone. Certain categories of conflict are common. By exploring some of these categories, we can start to recognize the seeds of conflict even before they sprout. We can then trigger new responses early, while the conflict is still small. In the activity sections of this book, we take children on journeys into conflicts they are likely to encounter in their worlds.

Opinions and Issues

We all have ideas about things. As an idea develops, it can rather quickly turn into an opinion. Sometimes we express opinions by saying things like, "The way I see it . . . " or "I believe . . . " Our opinions are formed from the raw materials of our belief systems. As an idea takes shape, it becomes an opinion based on what we believe.

We don't form our opinions by accident. Almost all opinions are formed in relation to an existing issue, an issue being any topic around which there are already at least two opinions. An issue can be very simple or very complex. For example, when two people each want to watch a different television program, we have one issue and two opinions. But when cable viewers debate the programming of a newly added channel, we have one main issue, several sub-issues, and thousands of opinions.

Opinions and issues are a good place to look to find conflicts. Whenever we express an opinion, we need to remember that we are likely to find at least one person who has a *different* opinion.

Some issues don't involve others. For example, let's say that Jack has to make a decision between going with friends to the fair and staying home to work on his taxes. In this case, Jack has two conflicting opinions based on entirely reasonable beliefs. On the one hand, Jack believes that refusing to go with his friends may jeopardize the friendship. Supporting this belief is the rationale that, even if he goes to the fair, he may still be able to devote a few late hours to his taxes. Finally, Jack believes that going out with friends will be good for him.

On the other hand, Jack believes that his friends will probably understand and respect a decision to stay home and work on taxes. Furthermore, Jack knows that taking care of the taxes will bolster his self-image. Finally, Jack believes that if he goes to the fair he'll put so much energy into dreading the work ahead and worrying about his deadline that he won't enjoy himself anyway.

Jack has two conflicting opinions based on two sets of beliefs. And as long as it continues unresolved, the conflict itself steals energy from both alternatives!

Similarities and Differences

Diversity also breeds conflict. People are fundamentally different simply by virtue of their belief systems. But they differ in many other ways, too. Here is an exercise we use in conflict-resolution workshops:

First, we ask participants to name all the ways they differ from one another. The answers come quickly, and include personality, preferences, skills, intelligence, traditions, culture, race, etc. In moments, we have a long list of differences.

Next, we ask participants to name all the ways they are *exactly* the same. This list is slow in forming. Usually someone says that they are all human beings. Someone else may suggest that they all have basic needs or that they are anatomically similar. This is where the second list generally stops.

At first glance, these two lists support the notion that people are different from one another, but we must pursue the question further.

We ask participants to think about the list of differences, and find a way to turn those differences into *exact* likenesses. Try it. Think about everyone having a *different* personality. Now put aside the "different" for a moment, and consider the fact that everyone *has* a personality, just as everyone has preferences, skills, intelligence, traditions, culture, race, etc. When we teach people to think about differences this way, they start to see how truly alike we are.

When we fail to see how much alike we are, we are planting the seeds of conflict. Focusing on the belief that we are different from one another actually *produces* conflict.

One Right Answer

A related ingredient that almost *always* produces conflict is the need to be RIGHT. If you and I are different and we both believe that only one of us is right, that automatically makes one of us wrong, and we have created a conflict over which of us holds title to the truth.

Learning to understand, respect, and appreciate similarities and differences is one key to resolving conflicts and is essential if we are to build on diversity and realize inclusion and interdependence. Unfortunately, most of us learn as children that there is only one right answer. From the moment we accept this fallacious notion, we close our minds to the ideas of other people, and limit ourselves to only one point of view. By recognizing that other answers have validity and value, we can expand our comfort zone and open ourselves to new information and personal growth.

Environments

Environments that are inconsistent with our belief systems produce another category of conflict. The writings of Carl Jung explain how temperament and personality influence the ways in which adults and children respond to various environmental conditions. Howard Gardner, in his book, *Frames of Mind*, reveals that children develop different kinds of intelligence that influence the way they respond to learning environments. Growing largely from genetic imprints and learned preferences, these intelligences also help shape the individual's belief system.

We bring our differences to every new environment. When the environment is consistent with our belief system, we feel comfortable and have a sense of well being. If we find ourselves in a dissonant environment . . . well, by now you know, we experience conflict.

Environmental conflicts come in all sizes—from the discomfort of sitting in a poorly-designed chair to the agony of conducting a meeting near an active demolition site. Many argue that environmental conflict is the primary cause of kids dropping out of school and adults burning out in their careers.

Turf

We begin to learn about possessions and territory from our earliest experiences. Collectively, possessions and territory comprise our "turf." Many cultures place a high premium on "getting" as a measure of success. A T-shirt reads, "He who dies with the most toys wins." A good question to ask is, "...wins what?"

Holding this belief, we move through life measuring our success by how much we obtain. We become acutely aware of intrusions and threats to our turf. When we lose something, we feel a discomfort akin to failure. If we lose enough, we may come to see *ourselves* as failures—a serious and destructive conclusion. It is very difficult to change an individual's identification with material possessions, but it is not so difficult to develop the skills necessary to constructively deal with conflicts involving turf.

When children learn to cooperate and work together collaboratively in teams, they start to recognize that the value of their turf also lies in its ability to contribute to a larger system.

Conflicts that arise from issues of turf can be small or global. When a neighbor's dog finds a handy place in the middle of our front yard to discharge a bodily function, we experience a small intrusion onto our turf. When we read of the rapid destruction of the rainforest, we are seeing a large intrusion onto our global turf. In the classroom, the turf issues of children are different, but no less important.

The habit of fixing blame is one we frequently bring to bear in conflict situations. We want to know who is responsible—who is the enemy. The truth is, one person may be responsible for starting the process of conflict, but all persons involved are responsible for resolving conflict in ways that produce a win for everyone.

Teaching the Skills of Conflict Resolution proposes that each of us use all of our resources to contribute to the success of those around us.

Consequences of Conflict

Every conflict produces a result or consequence. If we think of conflict as a process, we see that it invariably leads to a conclusion. Some conflicts are resolved very quickly, others may take a lifetime to resolve, but one way or another they all come to an end.

All conflicts produce change as a consequence. Since conflict is dynamic, change starts taking place the minute a conflict begins and doesn't end until it is resolved. For better or worse, when conflict begins, everything and everybody associated with it begins to change. The quality of the change produced by conflict is determined by the skill with which the conflict is managed and resolved.

Unmanaged Conflict Equals Destructive Resolution

A school is ripe with opportunity for conflict. From the farthest reaches of the playground to the most remote corner of the classroom, from student restrooms to the teacher's lounge, everything we've said about conflict holds true for schools.

Children bring to school the accumulation of everything they've learned—all of their habits and all the beliefs they've developed about themselves, other people, and their world. Such diversity makes conflict inevitable. And because the conflict-resolution skills of most children are poorly developed, the outcomes of conflict are frequently negative—at times even destructive.

Let's look at what children are likely to experience in the case of both internal and external conflict that is badly handled.

Internal conflict is the most difficult to deal with, because one of the unfortunate habits children develop is lack of trust. A conflict may fester and go unnoticed by everyone who could be of assistance. When this happens, a child may experience a variety of consequences—all negative. First, because the child is experiencing distress, not only is he or she distracted from learning, the neuro-mechanisms required for learning are rendered inoperable. In this condition, learning is impossible.

As the child struggles with this internal conflict, a sense of inadequacy starts to develop. The child is convinced that he or she is not capable of resolving the conflict. Looking about, the child perceives other children coping with everything in their lives. Little-by-little, self-esteem is eroded. The child develops a sense of vulnerability and may become isolated. He or she may lash out at those who offer assistance, interpreting their efforts as intrusions. Serious personal, social, and performance consequences may result, reinforcing past experiences and creating a cycle that can destroy a positive school experience.

This isn't a very happy picture, but it is happening throughout the U.S. It is happening in your school, and you may know children who are caught in this dilemma.

But doesn't internal conflict only affect the child? No. Because the child is out of the learning loop, the classroom teacher must give extra time, attention, and effort to working with the child so that he or she can keep abreast of the class. In many cases, this is an exercise in futility. When a class is disrupted because of one child's internal conflict, all students are affected. The demand for intensified classroom management further erodes teaching time, and the teacher experiences frustration, perhaps even a sense of failure.

If the teacher refers the child to a counselor, the time and energy of the counselor are now consumed, and if the problem persists, additional personnel must become involved. Thus, the energy being consumed is disproportionately larger than the initial conflict.

From Disagreement to Crisis

The results of external (or interpersonal) conflict are similar to those of internal conflict, but are usually broader because more people get involved.

External conflict between children usually begins with a disagreement. At this point, good conflict-resolution skills can have an immediate effect. More often than not, however, complications multiply and feelings escalate to the point where adult intervention is required. Disruptions caused by conflict spell disastrous consequences for learning. Time spent restoring peace is lost forever. Friendships and egos may be damaged, and the resulting tension in the classroom may further inhibit learning.

The most terrible consequence of external conflict is violence. When children do not have

the skills to resolve conflicts, they resort to whatever methods they've learned, often choosing aggression or complete withdrawal. At opposite ends of the response spectrum, aggression and withdrawal can be equally destructive. Aggression at its worst generates violent acts toward others; withdrawal and passivity at their worst generate violent acts toward the self.

A workable rule of thumb holds that the consequences of an unmanaged conflict are disproportionately larger than the conflict itself. We should keep this rule in mind when we are tempted to dismiss a child's conflict because we don't think it requires our attention. Nowhere in life is the adage "an ounce of prevention is worth a pound of cure" more applicable than in the realm of conflict.

Win-Lose and Lose-Lose

Over the years, we've heard a lot about win/ win, win/lose, and lose/lose. Our culture consistently places the highest value on winning, often at any cost. Sporting events of all kinds glorify winning and denigrate losing. We tend to carry over this attitude to the conflict arena, which is considerably more complicated. The only real choices in conflict are win/win and lose/lose. Win/lose is just another form of lose/ lose. Remember the Persian Gulf war? This global conflict had to do with issues, turf, and the need to be right. History records the Persian Gulf War as a win for the United Nations alliance headed by the United States, and a loss for Iraq—the classic win/lose scenario. However, a close look at the consequences of that conflict reveal something quite different. As the winner, the U.N. alliance spent billions of dollars, incurred a death toll in the hundreds of thousands, set off an environmental disaster of monumental proportions, and then restored the area to essentially the same level of instability that existed before the conflict, with Iraq behaving in a manner very like that which provoked the conflict in the first place.

In the final analysis, no one wins in a conflict unless everyone wins. *Teaching the Skills of Conflict Resolution* is dedicated to the premise that children *can* adopt a win/win spirit and *can* learn to effectively manage and resolve conflicts, and that the attitudes and skills required are transferable to every part of their lives for as long as they live.

Managed Conflict Equals Positive Change and Personal Growth

A goal of *Teaching the Skills of Conflict Resolution* is to prepare every child to recognize when he or she is experiencing a conflict and to know whether the conflict is internal or external in nature. With this awareness, the child can begin to identify resources to help resolve the conflict, and develop the skill and trust necessary to reach out to those resources.

Through collaboration with peers and adults at school, students are able to clearly define conflicts, and select or develop strategies for bringing about their resolution. Every time children engage in and resolve a conflict, they reinforce their skills and enhance their ability to constructively handle future conflict. Through peer mediation and other processes, the experience of actively helping one another further strengthens skill development. This promotes significant personal and social growth; students see themselves as capable of dealing effectively with conflict and interacting positively with others in the process. Self-esteem is enhanced, the need to belong is satisfied, and students experience a kind of bonding whose benefits transfer to other collaborative efforts such as cooperative learning.

For teachers, counselors, administrators, and parents, the rewards can be profound. Children who deal effectively with conflict bring significantly less stress to the classroom. They are better learners, demonstrate higher levels of cooperation, and require fewer interventions, thus conserving the teacher's time and energy. Counselors have fewer referrals and are free to be more effective resources. Administrators enjoy significant reductions in attention-sapping crises. For parents, the result is equally gratifying, as children perform at higher levels and start transferring conflict-resolution skills to the home.

All of these positive consequences occur when conflicts are well managed and skillfully resolved. In addition, schools experience greater inter-group harmony as students whose differences have caused them to polarize into athletic, ethnic, intellectual, and social groups begin to appreciate and value their similarities and differences.

The Win-Win Outcome

The ultimate outcome of *Teaching the Skills of Conflict Resolution* is a win/win climate in which all those who participate in a conflict and all those who are affected by it realize positive outcomes.

This scenario sounds so nice that it's hard to imagine anyone not wanting his or her students to learn these skills; still, two constraining factors must be addressed. They have nothing to do with children. Research and practical experience have demonstrated over and over again that wherever conflict resolution programs have been undertaken and sustained over periods of a year or more, significant results have been achieved.

The constraints are these: To effectively develop the skills of conflict resolution the curriculum *must be implemented*. Even if the activities are used only in a single classroom or by a single counselor, the effort must be made. Next, the program *must be sustained and consistently applied* in order for change to take place. Change takes time, but more importantly, it takes commitment. A degree of commitment sufficient to get the program started and keep it going till it becomes an integral, self-sustaining part of the classroom, if not the school. The positive and negative consequences of conflict are opposite sides of the same coin. Moving from one side to the other is not accomplished by flipping the coin, but by turning it over slowly. Take the time to understand and appreciate conflict and you'll make conflict resolution work!

An Overview of the Thematic Units

The materials in *Teaching the Skills of Conflict Resolution* are organized to focus on critical ingredients necessary to prevent conflict, and to successfully manage and resolve conflict when it occurs. Each unit begins with a brief introduction summarizing the outcomes targeted by the activities in the unit. This is followed by a section entitled, "Literature Connections," which lists the titles of thematically-related children's literature. Titles are suggested for primary-, intermediate- and upper-grade levels, and a brief synopsis of each book is provided.

The units in *Teaching the Skills of Conflict Resolution* serve as building blocks in a coherent curriculum for developing the skills and strategies of conflict prevention, management, and resolution. Following is a synopsis of each:

Respecting Similarities and Differences

One of the oldest sources of conflict is the lack of understanding between individuals and groups who are different with respect to such things as race, religion, appearance, life-style, cultural values, and physical or other disabilities. This unit helps students develop an awareness of characteristics they have in common with others, as well as attributes, talents, and beliefs that make them unique. Through the development of mutual understanding and respect, students begin to build a sound base for effectively dealing with conflict situations.

Understanding and Controlling Feelings

Emotional reactions are often born of deeply imbedded behavior patterns. When they catch us off guard, they can be frightening and difficult to accept. Children need to learn that their feelings are normal, predictable, and susceptible to control. In addition, feelings serve important purposes. Feelings convey messages about conditions and events going on around us in our environment. Feelings are closely linked to thoughts and provide important clues to the way the brain is processing information. Learning to understand feelings, control negative emotions, and express feelings appropriately are skills that keep conflicts in perspective, and enable children to begin managing conflict rather than being managed by it.

Communicating Effectively

Many potential conflicts can be avoided by communicating effectively. In addition, children who have learned to listen well and express themselves accurately are better able to deal effectively with conflict when it occurs. However, communicating in the stressful environment that usually accompanies conflict requires much greater skill than does normal communication. The activities in this unit have been designed to help children learn specific communication strategies that are crucial to creative and positive conflict resolution.

Cooperation and Teambuilding

Effective teams are characterized by interdependence and inclusion. Members are valued for their uniqueness. They trust one another, turn to each other for help and advice and, when they experience conflict, utilize positive methods to resolve it. Through activities that promote cooperation and teambuilding, children acquire many of the insights and skills necessary to interact effectively with their peers, to handle conflict, and to participate productively in collaborative projects and school assignments.

Strategies for Resolving Conflict

This unit presents familiar, common sense ways of dealing with conflict. The activities offer students the opportunity to become acquainted with a range of conflict management strategies, to discuss the relative pros and cons of those strategies, and to practice them safely through role playing and other forms of behavioral rehearsal.

Using the Tools of Conflict Resolution

By the time they reach this unit, students are equipped with a variety of skills and strategies for resolving conflict. The activities in this section are designed to transfer to students responsibility for choosing which strategy to use. In response to actual conflict situations, students are given many opportunities to prescribe strategies for themselves and their classmates, and to practice them repeatedly. Several peer mediation activities provide further reinforcement, and enrich the conflict repertoires of those students who wish to serve as third-party helpers. The transfer of learnings to real-life situations is the ultimate goal of this unit.

Putting It All Together

In this section you and your students are given opportunities to find broader application for the tools and strategies of conflict resolution through the examination of issues, problems, and conflicts in the community, nation, and world. The students brainstorm and evaluate various courses of action, and implement solutions by means of community action, letters to the editor, etc. With encouragement and practice, children can take everything they learn through this curriculum beyond the classroom and into the rest of their lives.

The Instructional Strategies

To achieve its goals, Teaching *the Skills of Conflict Resolution* incorporates a variety of proven instructional strategies. Activities include simulations, role plays, "experience sheets" for individual students to complete, and a host of small and large group activities and discussions. Many activities, particularly those in earlier units, focus on the prevention of conflict. Others deal with intervention strategies.

One of the most powerful and versatile of the instructional strategies used in this curriculum is the Sharing Circle. In each unit, two Sharing Circles are fully elaborated. These are followed by a list of additional Sharing Circle topics relevant to the goals of the unit. At first glance, the Sharing Circle—a small-group discussion process—is likely to appear deceptively simple. It is not. When used correctly, the Sharing Circle is unusually effective as a tool for developing awareness, insight, self-esteem, group cohesiveness, communication skills, and higher-level thinking. Please take the time to read the following sections before leading your first circle. Once you are familiar with the process, implement Sharing Circles regularly and as frequently as you can.

An Overview of the Sharing Circle

Twenty-five years of teaching the Sharing Circle process to educators world wide have demonstrated the power of the Sharing Circle in contributing to the development of conflict resolution skills. To take full advantage of this process there are some things you need to know.

First, the topic elaborations provided under the heading, "Introduce the Topic," in the two Sharing Circle examples in each unit are given as guides for you to use as you introduce other Sharing Circle topics from the lists you'll find at the end of each unit. Use this introduction to focus the attention of the students on the topic you are discussing.

In your elaboration, try to use language and examples that are appropriate to the age, ability, and culture of your students. In our examples, we have attempted to be as general as possible; however, those examples may not be the most appropriate for your students.

Second, we strongly urge you to respect the integrity of the sharing and discussion phases of the circle. These two phases are procedurally and qualitatively different, yet of equal importance in promoting awareness, insight, and higher-level thinking in students. The longer you lead Sharing Circles, the more you will appreciate the instructional advantages of maintaining this unique relationship.

All Sharing Circle topics are intended to develop awareness and insight through voluntary sharing. The discussion questions allow students to understand what has been shared at deeper levels, to evaluate ideas that have been generated by the topic, and to apply specific concepts to other areas of learning.

In order for students to lead fulfilling, productive lives, to interact effectively with others, and to become adept at resolving conflict, they first need to experience the fullness of themselves. They need to know who they are, how they function, and how they relate to others.

When used regularly, the *process* of the Sharing Circle coupled with its *content* (specific discussion topics) provides students with frequent opportunities to become more aware of their strengths, abilities, and positive qualities. In the Sharing Circle, students are listened to when they express their feelings and ideas, and they learn to listen to each other. The Sharing Circle format provides a framework in which genuine attention and acceptance can be given and received on a consistent basis.

By sharing their experiences and feelings in a safe environment, students are able to see basic commonalties among human beings— and individual differences, too. This understanding contributes to the development of self-respect. On a foundation of self-respect, students grow to understand and respect others.

As an instructional tool, the purpose of the Sharing Circle is to promote growth and development in students of all ages. Targeted growth areas include **communication, self-awareness, personal mastery,** and **interpersonal skills**. As students follow the rules and relate to each other verbally during the Sharing Circle, they are practicing oral communication and learning to listen. Through insights developed in the course of pondering and discussing the various topics, students are offered the opportunity to grow in awareness and to feel more masterful—more in control of

their feelings, thoughts, and behaviors. Through the positive experience of give and take, they learn more about effective modes of social interaction. This is a firm foundation upon which to build conflict resolution skills and strategies.

The Value of Listening

Many of us do not realize that merely listening to students talk can be immensely facilitating to their personal development. We do not need to diagnose, probe, or problem solve to help students focus attention on their own needs and use the information and insights in their own minds to arrive at their own conclusions. Because being listened to gives students confidence in their ability to positively affect their own lives, listening is certainly the helping method with the greatest long-term payoff.

When a student is dealing with a problem, or when her emotional state clearly indicates that something is bothering her, active listening is irreplaceable as a means of helping.

The Sharing Circle provides the opportunity for students to talk while others actively listen. By being given this opportunity, students gain important life skills and self-knowledge. Once they see that we do not intend to change them and that they may speak freely without threat of being "wrong," students find it easier to examine themselves and begin to see areas where they can make positive change in their lives. Just through the consistent process of sharing in a safe environment, students develop the ability to clarify their thoughts. They are encouraged to go deeper, find their own direction, and express and face strong feelings that may at other times be hidden obstacles to their growth. The important point is that students really can solve their own problems, develop self-awareness, and learn skills (including conflict resolution skills) that will enable them to become responsible members of society *if they are listened to effectively.*

Awareness

Words are the only tool we have for systematically turning our attention and awareness to the feelings within us, and for describing and reflecting on our thoughts and behaviors. Feelings, after all, lead people to marry, to seek revenge, to launch war, to create great works of art, and to commit their lives to the service of others. They are vital and compelling.

For students to be able to manage their feelings, they must know what those feelings are. To know what they are, they must practice describing them in words. When a particular feeling is grasped in words several times, the mind soon begins to automatically recall ideas and concepts in association with the feeling and can start to provide ways of dealing with the feeling; e.g., "I'm feeling angry and I need to get away from this situation to calm down."

With practice, the mind becomes more and more adept at making these connections. When a recognized feeling comes up, the mind can sort through alternative responses to the feeling. As a student practices this response sequence in reaction to a variety of feelings, he will find words floating into consciousness that accurately identify what is going on emotionally and physically for him. This knowledge in turn develops the capacity to think before and during action. One mark of maturity is the ability to recognize one's feelings and to take appropriate, responsible action. The more *immature* the student, the more his feelings rather than his thoughts determine his behavior. The ability to put words to feelings, to understand those words, to sort through an internal repertoire of responses and to choose appropriate, responsible behavior in reaction to a feeling indicates a high level of maturity and self-awareness.

By verbally exploring their own experiences in the circle and listening to others do the same, all in an environment of safety, students are gently and gradually prompted to explore deeper within themselves and to grow and expand in their understanding of others. As this mutual sharing takes place, they learn that feelings, thoughts, and behaviors are real and experienced by everyone. They see others succeeding and failing in the same kinds of ways they succeed and fail. They also begin to see each person as unique and to realize that they are unique, too. Out of this understanding, students experience a growing concern for others. A sense of responsibility develops as the needs, problems, values, and preferences of others penetrate their awareness.

Personal Mastery

Personal mastery can be defined as **self-confidence** together with **responsible competence**. Self-confidence is believing in oneself as a capable human being. Responsible competence is the willingness to take responsibility for one's actions coupled with the ability to demonstrate fundamental human relations skills (competencies).

Through participation in Sharing Circles, students are encouraged to explore their successes and hear positive comments about their efforts. Many Sharing Circle topics heighten students' awareness of their own successes and those of others. Failure, or falling short, is a reality that is also examined. The focus, however, is not to remind students that they have failed; instead these topics enable students to see that falling short is common and universal and is experienced by all people when they strive to accomplish things.

Sharing circle topics often address **human relations competencies**, such as the ability to include others, assume and share responsibility, offer help, behave assertively, solve problems, resolve conflicts, etc. Such topics elevate awareness in the human relations domain and encourage students to more effectively exercise these competencies and skills each day. The first step in a student's developing any competency is knowing that he or she is capable of demonstrating it. The Sharing Circle is particularly adept at helping students to recognize and acknowledge their own capabilities.

A particularly important element of personal mastery is **responsible competence**, or responsibility. By focusing on their positive behaviors and accomplishments, the attention of students is directed toward the internal and external rewards that can be gained when they behave responsibly.

The Sharing Circle is a wonderful tool for teaching cooperation. As equitably as possible, the circle structure attempts to meet the needs of all participants. Everyone's feelings are accepted. Comparisons and judgements are not made. The circle is not another competitive arena, but is guided by a spirit of collaboration. When students practice fair, respectful interaction with one another, they benefit from the experience and are likely to employ these responsible behaviors in other life situations.

Interpersonal Skills

Relating effectively to others is a challenge we all face. People who are effective in their social interactions have the ability to understand others. They know how to interact flexibly, skillfully, and responsibly. At the same time, they recognize their own needs and maintain their own integrity. Socially effective people can process the nonverbal as well as verbal messages of others. They possess the very important awareness that all people have the power to affect one another. They are aware of not only how others affect them, but the effects their behaviors have on others which is vital in conflict resolution.

The Sharing Circle process has been designed so that healthy, responsible behaviors are modeled by the teacher or counselor in his or her role as circle leader. The rules also require that the students relate positively and effectively to one another. The Sharing Circle brings out and affirms the positive qualities inherent in everyone and allows students to practice effective modes of communication. Because Sharing Circles provide a place where participants are listened to and their feelings accepted, students learn how to provide the same conditions to peers and adults outside the circle.

One of the great benefits of the Sharing Circle is that it does not merely *teach* young people about social interaction, it lets them *interact*! Every Sharing Circle is a real-life experience of social interaction where the stu-dents share, listen, explore, plan, dream, and problem solve together. As they interact, they learn about each other and they realize what it takes to relate effectively to others. Any given Sharing Circle may provide a dozen tiny flashes of positive interpersonal insight for an individual participant. Gradually, the reality of what constitutes effective behavior in relating to others is internalized.

Through this regular sharing of interpersonal experiences, the students learn that behavior can be positive or negative, and sometimes both at the same time. Consequences can be constructive, destructive, or both. Different people respond differently to the same event. They have different feelings and thoughts. The students begin to understand what will cause what to happen; they grasp the concept of cause and effect; they see themselves affecting others and being affected *by* others.

The ability to make accurate interpretations and responses in social interactions allows students to know where they stand with themselves and with others. They can tell what actions "fit" a situation. Sharing Circles are marvelous testing grounds where students can observe themselves and others in action, and can begin to see themselves as contributing to the good and bad feelings of others. With this understanding, students are helped to conclude that being responsible towards others feels good, and is the most valuable and personally rewarding form of interaction.

Sharing Circles can noticeably accelerate the development and internalization of the conflict resolution skills and strategies introduced in this book. They are a key ingredient in bringing about the growth necessary for students to engage in the level of *self*-management required to effectively manage and resolve conflict.

How to Set Up Sharing Circles

Group Size and Composition

Sharing Circles are a time for focusing on individuals' contributions in an unhurried fashion. For this reason, each circle session group needs to be kept relatively small—eight to twelve usually works best. Once they move beyond the primary grades, students are capable of extensive verbalization. You will want to encourage this, and not stifle them because of time constraints.

Each group should be as **heterogeneous** as possible with respect to sex, ability, and racial/ethnic background. Sometimes there will be a group in which all the students are particularly reticent to speak. At these times, bring in an expressive student or two who will get things going. Sometimes it is necessary for practical reasons to change the membership of a group. Once established, however, it is advisable to keep a group as stable as possible.

Length and Location of Sharing Circles

Most circle sessions last approximately 20 to 30 minutes. At first students tend to be reluctant to express themselves fully because they do not yet know that the circle is a safe place. Consequently your first sessions may not last more than 10 to 15 minutes. Generally speaking, students become comfortable and motivated to speak with continued experience.

In middle-school classrooms circle sessions may be conducted at any time during the class period. Starting circle sessions at the beginning of the period allows additional time in case students become deeply involved in the topic. If you start circles late in the period, make sure the students are aware of their responsibility to be concise.

In elementary classes, any time of day is appropriate for Sharing Circles. Some teachers like to set the tone for the day by beginning with circles; others feel it's a perfect way to complete the day and to send the children away with positive feelings.

Circle sessions may be carried out wherever there is room for students to sit in a circle and experience few or no distractions. Most leaders prefer to have students sit in chairs rather than on the floor. Students seem to be less apt to invade one another's space while seated in chairs. Some leaders conduct sessions outdoors, with students seated in a secluded, grassy area.

How to Get Started With Sharing Circles

Teachers and counselors have used numerous methods to involve students in the circle process. What works well for one leader or class does not always work for another. Here are two basic strategies leaders have successfully used to get groups started. Whichever you use, we recommend that you post a chart listing the circle session rules and procedures to which every participant may refer.

1. Start one group at a time, and cycle through all groups. If possible, provide an opportunity for every student to experience a circle session in a setting where there are no disturbances. This may mean arranging for another staff member or aide to take charge of the students not participating in the circle. Non-participants may work on course work or silent reading, or, if you have a cooperative librarian, they may be sent to the library to work independently or in small groups on a class assignment. Repeat this procedure until

all of the students have been involved in at least one circle session.

Next, initiate a class discussion about the circle sessions. Explain that from now on you will be meeting with each circle group in the classroom, with the remainder of the class present. Ask the students to help you plan established procedures for the remainder of the class to follow.

Meet with each circle session group on a different day, systematically cycling through the groups.

2. Combine inner and outer circles. Meet with one circle session group while another group listens and observes as an outer circle. Then have the two groups change places, with the students on the outside becoming the inner circle, and responding verbally to the topic. If you run out of time in middle-school classrooms, use two class periods for this. Later, a third group may be added to this alternating cycle. The end product of this arrangement is two or more groups (comprising everyone in the class) meeting together simultaneously. While one group is involved in discussion, the other groups listen and observe as members of an outer circle. *Invite the members of the outer circle to participate in the review and discussion phases of the circle.*

What To Do With the Rest of the Class

A number of arrangements can be made for students who are not participating in circle sessions. Here are some ideas:

- **Arrange the room to ensure privacy.** This may involve placing a circle of chairs or carpeting in a corner, away from other work areas. You might construct dividers from existing furniture, such as bookshelves or screens, or simply arrange chairs and tables in such a way that the circle area is protected from distractions.
- **Involve aides, counselors, parents, or fellow teachers.** Have an aide conduct a lesson with the rest of the class while you meet with a circle group. If you do not have an aide assigned to you, use auxiliary staff or parent volunteers.
- **Have students work quietly on subject-area assignments in pairs or small, task-oriented groups.**
- **Utilize student aides or leaders.**

If the seat-work activity is in a content area, appoint students who show ability in that area as "consultants," and have them assist other students.

- **Give the students plenty to do.** List academic activities on the board. Make materials for quiet individual activities available so that students cannot run out of things to do and be tempted to consult you or disturb others.
- **Make the activity of students outside the circle enjoyable.** When you can involve the rest of the class in something meaningful to them, students will probably be less likely to interrupt the circle.
- **Have the students work on an ongoing project.** When they have a task in progress, students can simply resume where they left off, with little or no introduction from you. In these cases, appointing a "person in charge," "group leader," or "consultant" is wise.
- **Allow individual journal-writing.** While a circle is in progress, have the other students make entries in a private (or share-with-teacher-only) journal. The topic for journal writing could be the same topic that is being discussed in the Sharing Circle. Do not correct the journals, but if you read them, be sure to respond to the entries with your own written thoughts, where appropriate.

Leading the Sharing Circle

This section is a thorough guide for conducting Sharing Circles. It covers major points to keep in mind and answers questions which will arise as you begin using the program. Please remember that these guidelines are presented to assist you, not to restrict you. Follow them and trust your own leadership style at the same time.

Sharing Circle Procedures for the Leader

1. Setting up the circle (1-2 minutes)
2. Reviewing the ground rules (1-2 minutes) *
3. Introducing the topic (1-2 minutes)
4. Sharing by circle members (12-18 minutes)
5. Reviewing what is shared (3-5 minutes) **
6. Summary discussion (2-8 minutes)
7. Closing the circle (less than 1 minute)

*optional after the first few sessions
**optional

Setting up the circle (1-2 minutes)

As you sit down with the students in the circle, remember that you are not teaching a lesson. You are facilitating a group of people. Establish a positive atmosphere. In a relaxed manner, address each student by name, using eye contact and conveying warmth. An attitude of seriousness blended with enthusiasm will let the students know that the circle session is an important learning experience—an activity that can be interesting and meaningful.

Reviewing the ground rules (1-2 minutes).

At the beginning of the first session, and at appropriate intervals thereafter, go over the rules for the circle session. They are:

Sharing Circle Rules

1. Bring yourself to the circle and nothing else.
2. Everyone gets a turn to share, including the leader.
3. You can skip your turn if you wish.
4. Listen to the person who is sharing.
5. The time is shared equally.
6. Stay in your own space.
7. There are no interruptions, probing, put-downs, or gossip.

From this point on, demonstrate to the students that you expect them to remember and abide by the ground rules. Convey that you think well of them and know they are fully capable of responsible behavior. Let them know that by coming to the session they are making a commitment to listen and show acceptance and respect for the other students and you.

Introducing the topic (1-2 minutes)

State the topic in your own words. Elaborate and provide examples as each activity suggests. Add clarifying statements of your own that will help the students understand the topic. Answer questions about the topic, and emphasize that there are no "right" responses. Finally, restate the topic, opening the session to responses (theirs and yours). Sometimes taking your turn first helps the students understand the aim of the topic. At various points throughout the session, state the topic again.

Just prior to leading a circle session, contemplate the topic and think of at least one possible response that *you* can make to it.

Sharing by circle members (12-18 minutes)

The most important point to remember is this: The purpose of the circle session is to give students an opportunity to express themselves and be accepted for the experiences, thoughts, and feelings they share. Avoid taking the action away from the circle members. They are the stars!

Reviewing what is shared (optional 3-5 minutes)

Besides modeling effective listening (the very best way to teach it) and positively reinforcing students for attentive listening, a review can be used to deliberately improve listening skills in circle members.

Reviewing is a time for reflective listening, when circle members feed back what they heard each other say during the sharing phase of the circle. Besides encouraging effective listening, reviewing provides circle members with additional recognition. It validates their experience and conveys the idea, "you are important," a message we can all profit from hearing often.

To review, a circle member simply addresses someone who shared, and briefly paraphrases what the person said ("John, I heard you say....").

The first few times you conduct reviews, stress the importance of checking with the speaker to see if the review accurately summarized the main things that were shared. If the speaker says, "No," allow him or her to make corrections. Stress too, the importance of speaking *directly* to the speaker, using the person's name and the pronoun "you," not "he" or "she." If someone says, "She said that...," intervene as promptly and respectfully as possible and say to the reviewer, "Talk to Betty...Say you." This is very important. The person whose turn is being reviewed will have a totally different feeling when talked *to*, instead of *about*.

Note: Remember that the review is optional and is most effective when used *occasionally*, not as a part of every circle.

Summary discussion (2-8 minutes)

The summary discussion is the cognitive portion of the circle session. During this phase, the leader asks thought-provoking questions to stimulate free discussion and higher-level thinking. The two Sharing Circle examples in each unit include summary questions and may be used as guides as you formulate your own questions for the list of Sharing Circle topics provided in each unit. As you develop these summary discussion questions, keep in mind the level of understanding of your students and on what specific learning you would like them to focus. You may also choose to ask questions related directly to what was actually shared in the circle.

It is important that you not confuse the summary with the review. The review is optional; the summary is not. The summary meets the need of people of all ages to find meaning in what they do. Thus, the summary serves as a necessary culmination to each circle session by allowing the students to clarify the key concepts they gained from the session.

Closing the circle (less than 1 minute).

The ideal time to end a circle session is when the summary discussion reaches natural closure. Sincerely thank everyone for being part of the circle. Don't thank specific students for speaking, as doing so might convey the impression that speaking is more appreciated than mere listening. Then close the circle by saying, "The circle session is over," or "OK, that ends our session."

More about Sharing Circle Procedures and Rules

The next few paragraphs offer further clarification concerning circle session leadership.

Why should students bring themselves to the circle and nothing else? Individual teachers differ on this point, but most prefer that students not bring objects (such as pencils, books, etc.) to the circle that may be distracting.

Who gets to talk? Everyone. The importance of acceptance in Sharing Circles cannot be overly stressed. In one way or another practically every ground rule says one thing: *accept one another.* When you model acceptance of students, they will learn how to be accepting. Each individual in the circle is important and deserves a turn to speak if he or she wishes to take it. Equal opportunity to become involved should be given to everyone in the circle.

Circle members should be reinforced equally for their contributions. There are many reasons why a leader may become more enthused over what one student shares than another. The response may be more on target, reflect more depth, be more entertaining, be philosophically more in keeping with one's own point of view, and so on. However, students need to be given equal recognition for their contributions, even if the contribution is to listen silently throughout the session.

In most of the circle sessions, plan to take a turn and address the topic, too. Students usually appreciate it very much and learn a great deal when their teachers and counselors are willing to tell about their own experiences, thoughts, and feelings. In this way you let your students know that you acknowledge your own humanness.

Does everyone have to take a turn? No. Students may choose to skip their turns. If the circle becomes a pressure situation in which the members are coerced in any way to speak, it will become an unsafe place where participants are not comfortable. Meaningful discussion is unlikely in such an atmosphere. By allowing students to make this choice, you are showing them that you accept their right to remain silent if that is what they choose to do.

As you begin circles, it will be to your advantage if one or more students decline to speak. If you are imperturbable and accepting when this happens, you let them know you are offering them an opportunity to experience something you think is valuable, or at least worth a try, and not attempting to force-feed them. You as a leader should not feel compelled to share a personal experience in every session, either. However, if you decline to speak in most of the sessions, this may have an inhibiting effect on the students' willingness to share.

A word should also be said about how this ground rule has sometimes been carried to extremes. Sometimes leaders have bent over backwards to let students know they don't have to take a turn. This seeming lack of enthusiasm on the part of the leader has caused reticence in the students. In order to avoid this outcome, don't project any personal insecurity as you lead the session. Be confident in your proven ability to work with students. Expect something to happen and it will.

Some circle leaders ask the participants to raise their hands when they wish to speak, while others simply allow free verbal sharing without soliciting the leader's permission first. Choose the procedure that works best for you, but do not call on anyone unless you can see signs of readiness.

Some leaders have reported that their first circles fell flat—that no one, or just one or two students, had anything to say. But they continued to have circles, and at a certain point everything changed. Thereafter, the students had a great deal to say that these leaders considered worth waiting for. It appears that in these cases the leaders' acceptance of the right to skip turns was a key factor. In time most students will contribute verbally when they have something they want to say, and when they are assured there is no pressure to do so.

Sometimes a silence occurs during a circle

session. Don't feel you have to jump in every time someone stops talking. During silences students have an opportunity to think about what they would like to share or to contemplate an important idea they've heard. A general rule of thumb is to allow silence to the point that you observe group discomfort. At that point move on. *Do not switch to another topic.* To do so implies you will not be satisfied until the students speak. If you change to another topic, you are telling them you didn't really mean it when you said they didn't have to take a turn if they didn't want to.

If you are bothered about students who attend a number of circles and still do not share verbally, reevaluate what you consider to be involvement. Participation does not necessarily mean talking. Students who do not speak *are* listening and learning.

How can I encourage effective listening? The Sharing Circle is a time (and place) for students and leaders to strengthen the habit of listening by doing it over and over again. No one was born knowing how to listen effectively to others. It is a skill like any other that gets better as it is practiced. In the immediacy of the circle session, the members become keenly aware of the necessity to listen, and most students respond by expecting it of one another.

In the Sharing Circle, listening is defined as the respectful focusing of attention on individual speakers. It includes eye contact with the speaker and open body posture. It eschews interruptions of any kind. When you conduct a circle session, listen and encourage listening in the students by (1) focusing your attention on the person who is speaking, (2) being receptive to what the speaker is saying (not mentally planning your next remark), and (3) recognizing the speaker when she finishes speaking, either verbally ("Thanks, Shirley") or non-verbally (a nod and a smile).

To encourage effective listening in the students, reinforce them by letting them know you have noticed they were listening to each other and you appreciate it. Occasionally conducting a review after the sharing phase also has the effect of sharpening listening skills.

How can I ensure the students get equal time? When circle members share the time equally, they demonstrate their acceptance of the notion that everyone's contribution is of equal importance. It is not uncommon to have at least one dominator in a group. This person is usually totally unaware that by continuing to talk he or she is taking time from others who are less assertive.

Be very clear with the students about the purpose of this ground rule. Tell them at the outset how much time there is and whether or not you plan to conduct a review. When it is your turn, always limit your own contribution. If someone goes on and on, do intervene (dominators need to know what they are doing), but do so as gently and respectfully as you can.

What are some examples of put-downs? Put-downs convey the message, "You are not okay as you are." Some put-downs are deliberate, but many are made unknowingly. Both kinds are undesirable in a Sharing Circle because they destroy the atmosphere of acceptance and disrupt the flow of discussion. Typical put-downs include:

- overquestioning.
- statements that have the effect of teaching or preaching
- advice giving
- one-upsmanship
- criticism, disapproval, or objections
- sarcasm
- statements or questions of disbelief

How can I deal with put-downs? There are two major ways for dealing with put-downs in circle sessions: preventing them from occurring and intervening when they do.

Going over the ground rules with the students at the beginning of each session, particularly in the earliest sessions, is a helpful preventive technique. Another is to reinforce the students when they adhere to the rule. Be sure to use nonpatronizing, nonevaluative language.

Unacceptable behavior should be stopped the moment it is recognized by the leader. When you become aware that a put-down is occurring, do whatever you ordinarily do to stop destructive behavior in the classroom. If one student gives another an unasked-for bit of advice, say for example, "Jane, please give Alicia a chance to tell her story." To a student who interrupts say, "Ed, it's Sally's turn." In most cases the fewer words, the better—students automatically tune out messages delivered as lectures.

Sometimes students disrupt the group by starting a private conversation with the person next to them. Touch the offender on the arm or shoulder while continuing to give eye contact to the student who is speaking. If you can't reach the offender, simply remind him or her of the rule about listening. If students persist in putting others down during circle sessions, ask to see them at another time and hold a brief one-to-one conference, urging them to follow the rules. Suggest that they reconsider their membership in the circle. Make it clear that if they don't intend to honor the ground rules, they are not to come to the circle.

How can I keep students from gossiping? Periodically remind students that using names and sharing embarrassing information is not acceptable. Urge the students to relate personally to one another, but not to tell intimate details of their lives.

What should the leader do during the summary discussion? Conduct the summary as an open forum, giving students the opportunity to discuss a variety of ideas and accept those that make sense to them. Don't impose your opinions on the students, or allow the students to impose theirs on one another. Ask open-ended questions, encourage higher-level thinking, contribute your own ideas when appropriate, and act as a facilitator.

Peer Mediation

Teaching the Skills of Conflict Resolution serves as an excellent resource when preparing students to participate in any one of a number of peer mediation programs currently available. Most published peer-mediation programs provide excellent guidelines for planning and organizing such an effort. Use this curriculum to add value to your chosen program by constructing a foundation of communication skills, conflict-resolution strategies, and process tools. If you are interested in developing a peer mediation program, here are some suggestions:

PEER MEDIATION—Conflict Resolution in Schools, by Fred Schrumpf, Donna Crawford, and H. Chu Usadel is published by Research Press Company, Champaign, Illinois.

Peer Counseling, by H. D. Gray and J. Tindall is published by Accelerated Development, Inc., Muncie, Indiana.

Caring and Sharing: Becoming a Peer Facilitator and *Youth Helping Youth*, by Robert D. Myrick and T. Erney are published by Educational Media Corporation, Minneapolis, Minnesota.

The Complete Handbook of Peer Counseling by D. Samuels and M. Samuels is published by Fiesta Publishing Corp., Miami, Florida.

Children Helping Children by Robert D. Myrick and Robert P. Bowman is published by Educational Media Corporation, Minneapolis, Minnesota.

Respecting Similarities and Differences

One of the purposes of this book is to help you *prevent* conflict among your students through the development of mutual understanding and respect.

As is sometimes painfully apparent in our adult world, one of the oldest sources of conflict and the most difficult to mediate is conflict based not on anything substantive or tangible, but on a lack of understanding among individuals and groups who are different with respect to such things as race, religion, appearance, lifestyle, cultural values, and physical disability.

People who are like us fit more easily within our comfort zone than do people who are different. We are jarred by differences; we feel threatened. If life is a contest to be "right," then to be convinced that our way is right, we must somehow rationalize that the other person wrong. Even when we accept that such behavior is indefensible, we resist stepping outside our comfort zone and we also resist extending its boundaries.

Children have a healthy curiosity about differences and they want to understand their world, but if no concerted effort is made to provide understanding, they will soon adopt the fears and prejudices of the adults around them. By the time

kids are approaching adolescence, when conformity with the group becomes a predominant preoccupation, if the comfort zone hasn't grown large enough to include a pretty diverse group, the seeds of this type of conflict will rapidly take root.

To develop mutual understanding and respect, students must have regular opportunities to talk about their commonalties and uniquenesses. They need to learn to value the different backgrounds and experiences that each of them brings to the classroom. They also need to develop a capacity for empathy by examining what it feels like to be discriminated against. Therefore, in this section you will find activities that are designed to help students:
- identify the gifts and talents of each member of the class.
- recognize how they as individuals and the class as a whole benefit from each person's background and special abilities.
- understand that people come from different and sometimes difficult circumstances.
- develop empathy.
- examine the roots and meaning of prejudice.
- respect one another's perceptions, likes, and dislikes.
- learn the value of inclusion.

Literature Connections

The following list of children's literature is offered to augment the activities in this section. An effective approach would be to ask the students to read one or more of the books prior to beginning the activities. If your students are very young, read the books aloud in class. In both cases, generate discussion by asking open-ended questions designed to reinforce understanding of the concepts conveyed through the story.

Primary:

Surat, Michele Maria, *Angel Child, Dragon Child*, illustrated by Vo-Dinh Mai, Carnival/Raintree, 1983

In this story, a Vietnamese girl named Ut enters an American school for the first time. After a conflict with a red-haired boy, who teases her for the white pajamas she wears to school and the funny words she speaks, Ut is forced to communicate with him. They become fast friends, and the red-haired boy decides to help Ut's family get the money to bring her mother to the United States by suggesting that the school put on a Vietnamese fair.

Friedman, Ina, *How My Parents Learned to Eat*, illustrated by Alan Say, Houghton Mifflin, 1984.

A young girl narrates this story, explaining why some days her family eats with chopsticks and some days they eat with knives and forks. She recounts the courtship of her American sailor father and her Japanese mother.

Intermediate:

Little, Jean, *From Anna*, illustrated by Joan Sandin, HarperCollins, 1972.

Nine-year-old Anna Solden and her family leave fascist Germany for Canada in 1933. Dubbed "Awkward Anna" by her siblings, she cannot read and write. It's not until a Canadian doctor examines her that her family realizes she is seriously sight impaired. She is finally helped by a supportive teacher and classmates when placed in a special sight-saving class.

Cohen, Barbara, *Molly's Pilgrim*, illustrated by Michael Deraney, Lothrup, Lee & Shepard, 1983.

Molly is unhappy about living in a small town in America because she is embarrassed by her clothes, uncertain about her English, and teased by her classmates. When Molly's class makes pilgrim dolls for Thanksgiving, her Jewish mother dresses Molly's doll as she was dressed before leaving Russia to seek religious freedom. The class learns from Molly and her teacher that there are modern pilgrims, too.

Upper:

Lord, Bette Bao, *In the Year of the Boar and Jackie Robinson*, illustrated by Marc Simont, Harper & Row, 1984.

Set in 1947, the story is about a young Chinese immigrant, Shirley Temple Wong, who finds it difficult to adjust to her new life until she discovers baseball and her hero, Jackie Robinson, the star of the Brooklyn Dodgers.

L'Engle, Madeleine, *A Wrinkle in Time*, Farrar, Straus and Giroux, 1962.

This science fiction adventure stars Meg Murray and her precocious little brother, Charles Wallace. Both are mentally gifted with a set of scientist parents, but Meg does not succeed academically or socially at school and five-year-old Charles Wallace won't even talk when he's around strangers. They set off to find and rescue their father, and find the power of love, which is stronger than all other mental gifts.

We All Have Talents
Writing, Sharing, and Discussion

Objectives:

The students will:
— describe their unique abilities and talents.
— acknowledge the abilities and talents of classmates.
— demonstrate understanding of the concept, "strength in diversity."

Grades:

1-8

Materials:

one copy of the experience sheet, "My Special Gifts and Talents," and writing materials for each student

Procedure:

Introduce the activity by asking the students to think about talents or "gifts" that they possess. Explain that a talent or gift is a special ability, like the ability to play a musical instrument or to draw pictures, or speak another language. Some people have a talent for math, science, or history; others are gifted at making friends or playing a particular sport. A gift or talent can be almost anything a person does well. Describe to the students two or three gifts or talents that *you* possess.

Distribute the experience sheet, "My Special Gifts and Talents." Have the students record their name at the top of the sheet, and then write down as many of their own gifts/talents as they can think of. While the students are working, circulate and offer help and suggestions as needed. Ensure that every child identifies and records several gifts/talents.

When they have completed their experience sheets, ask the students to look over what they have written, and circle one talent that they would feel comfortable describing to their classmates. Then have the students form groups of

four to six, and take turns sharing their thoughts and feelings about their identified talent.

Discussion Questions:

Have the students return to their seats for a general discussion. Ask these and other questions:

1. What is a gift or talent? How can you recognize your own talents?
2. How are our gifts and talents the same? How are they different?
4. What would the world be like if everyone had exactly the same gifts and talents?
5. What would happen if everyone on a football team were a talented passer, but no one had a talent for blocking, kicking, catching, running, or calling plays?
6. How can we use our individual talents and abilities to make our class a better place to learn?

Grades 1-5: Tell the students to keep their experience sheets for use in another activity. Follow this activity with the one entitled, "Linked Together."

My Special Gifts and Talents

My name is, _____ , and I bring
these special gifts and talents to my classroom:

1. _____

   _____

2. _____

   _____

3. _____

   _____

4. _____

   _____

5. _____

   _____

Linked Together
Creating a Classroom Chain

Objectives:

The students will:
—describe a unique gift/talent they possess.
—verbally and nonverbally acknowledge the gifts/talents of classmates.
—demonstrate understanding that strength exists in diversity.

Grades:

1-5

Materials:

one copy of the experience sheet, "Chain Link," for each student; crayons or magic markers; glue and scissors

Procedure:

Ask the students to take out their experience sheet, "My Special Gifts and Talents" and look again at what they wrote. Briefly review by asking volunteers to read aloud the gift/talent they circled and to recall the talent of one other student. Continue until at least a dozen different talents have been mentioned.

Next, ask the students to recall and reiterate the reasons why it is important for a team to value and utilize the unique gifts and talents of all its members. Ask the students to explain how utilizing everyone's gifts and talents can make the classroom a better place to learn and grow.

In your own words, explain that the strength and unity within a class can be compared to a chain with many individual links. If each link represents a different strength, uniting the links creates a chain that is longer and much stronger than any single link could ever be alone. Similarly, uniting gifts and talents in the classroom makes the group stronger by allowing every individual to benefit from the strength of every other individual. Ask the students to comment and to share their own ideas and insights.

Distribute the "Chain Link" experience sheets along with the crayons or magic markers. Have the students write their name and talent in the spaces provided. (Demonstrate by preparing a link of your own to add to the chain.) Instruct the students to cut out their link and decorate both sides. Finally, have the students work together to join the links with glue, forming a single chain. Have them hang the chain in an appropriate place within the classroom.

In a brief follow-up discussion, ask the students to talk about what they learned from the activity.

Chain Link

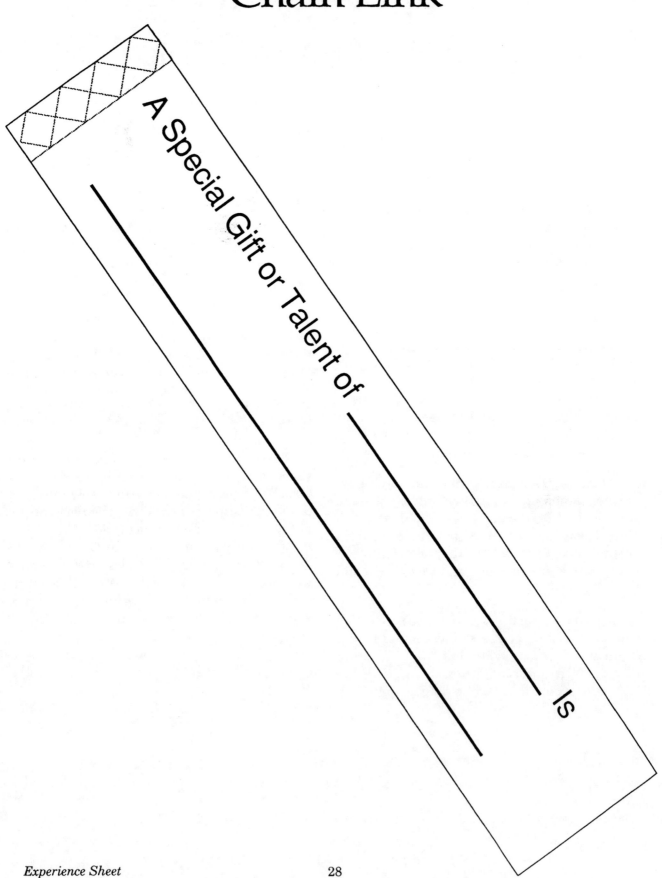

A Special Gift or Talent of _____ is _____

Reaching Out
Stories and Discussion

Objectives:
The students will:
— recognize and describe the feelings of others.
— demonstrate understanding of the needs of people who are different from themselves.
— state that the perceptions of people may differ, even when the thing perceived is the same.
— explain that all people, including those who are culturally and physically different from one another, share the same kinds of feelings.

Grades:
1-8

Materials:
writing materials for older students; art materials for younger students

Procedure:
Choose one (or more) of the following stories and read it to the students. In your own words, say: *I'm going to read you a short story. I'd like your help in thinking of some solutions to the problem that the person in the story is experiencing.*

After reading the story, facilitate a class discussion using the questions provided. After the discussion, ask each student to write his or her own ending to the story (or to one of the stories, if you read several). If your students are very young, you may prefer to have them draw a picture illustrating a positive conclusion. Ask the students to share their story endings or illustrations with the class.

Jamil's First Day of School
Jamil entered his first-grade classroom as a non-English speaker, having just arrived from the Philippines. He had never been in a school before and, on his first day, he began running around the classroom making noises. When the teacher told him to sit down, he didn't understand what she said and continued to make silly humming sounds. The other children began to laugh and started to make noises, too. The teacher scolded the children, and said that they would have to give up 5 minutes of their recess to discuss their behavior. During the discussion, the teacher explained that Jamil did not understand English and never learned appropriate school behavior. She asked the children to help Jamil become a successful school citizen.

Discussion Questions:
1. How do you think Jamil felt being a new boy in the class?
2. How do you think Jamil felt not understanding what anyone said?
3. What could you do to help Jamil understand good school behavior?
4. What could Jamil have done to help the other children learn about his life in the Philippines?
5. How could you be Jamil's friend and help him learn English words?

Karla's Ordeal

Nine-year-old Karla tried to make friends at every school she attended, and this was the third school in the past year. But the other girls made fun of her old clothes and sometimes unbrushed hair and dirty face. Karla lived with her dad and two brothers in an old camper. They moved from one trailer park to another, in whatever town her father could find work. The camper had no running water, so Karla had to use the trailer-park bathrooms, which sometimes had neither showers nor hot water. At school, the children called her "Homeless Orphan" on the playground. "I am not homeless. I live in a trailer with my dad, who calls me his princess," Karla would answer. Finally, one of the older girls, overhearing the name-calling, shouted to the others, "Come on. Quit teasing Karla. She's the best artist in the school. I saw her pictures on the cafeteria bulletin board!"

Discussion Questions:

1. How do you think Karla felt when the other girls teased her?
2. Why do you think the older girl tried to defend Karla by shouting to the ones who were teasing her?
3. What could Karla have done to try to make friends with the girls who were teasing her?
4. What could the other girls have done to help Karla when she came to school with a dirty face?

Why Jerome Won't Talk

Jerome loved attending Scouts when they played outdoor games, made things out of wood or paper, or went hiking. He could run fast, catch balls, and make things with his hands better than most of the other boys. But when it came time to say the Scout promise or join in group discussions, Jerome wouldn't participate. Every time he tried to speak, he began to stutter, "I p-p-p-promise to d-d-do..." Jerome usually quit before he finished a sentence. Often, some of the boys put their hands over their mouths and giggled. Jerome saw this and he stopped even trying to speak. The Scout leader tried to encourage him to speak, "Come on, Jerome. Keep trying. It doesn't have to be perfect." But Jerome just looked down, silently.

Discussion Questions:

1. How do you think Jerome felt about stuttering when he talked?
2. How do you think Jerome felt when the boys giggled?
3. What could the boys have done to help him?
4. What could Jerome have done to make friends with the boys?

A Test of Friendship

Naomi and Lisa became good friends in the sixth grade. They were in the same class at school and lived in apartment buildings on the same city block. The girls took violin lessons together after school and played on the neighborhood soccer team. They often slept over at each other's apartments, and sometimes ate dinner with each other's families. The only problems the girls encountered in their friendship occurred on holidays, especially during the winter. Naomi was Jewish and celebrated holy days with her family, at home and in the synagogue. During Hanukkah in December, Naomi wanted to stay home with her family to light the candles on their menorah and play games with the dreidl. Lisa wanted Naomi to spend the night with her and decorate her family's Christmas tree. The girls had a big argument over this, which almost ruined their friendship.

Discussion Questions:

1. How do you think the girls could have solved their problem?
2. What could the girls' families have done to help them solve their problem?
3. How could the girls have used their differences to strengthen their friendship?

Learning About Each Other
Team Talk

Objectives:

The students will:
— recognize and describe their own worth and worthiness.
— identify strengths, talents, and special abilities in self and others.
— practice methods of positive self-talk.
— describe similarities and differences among classmates.

Grades:

3-8

Materials:

selected dyad topics (provided on the next page) listed on the chalkboard

---

Procedure:

Have the students form teams of two and sit facing each other. Announce that the dyad members are going to take turns talking to each other about a series of topics. In your own words, explain: *Each person will have two minutes to speak to the topic while the other person listens. The person talking should try to be as open and clear as he or she can be. The person listening should be as good a listener as possible, focusing on the speaker rather than paying attention to other things in the room or to personal thoughts. The listener must not interrupt the speaker for any reason while he or she is talking.*

Select several topics that are appropriate for the age range of your class, and write them on the board. Begin the sequence with the first topic and call time after 2 minutes. Have the students switch roles and address the same topic again. Follow the same procedure for the remaining topics.

When all the topics have been discussed, ask the dyads to stand up and join another pair of students, forming groups of four. Direct each person in the group to introduce his/her partner to the new pair by telling them something about the partner that was learned during the dyad sequence. Allow time for one complete round of introductions, then break the groups of four into the original dyads and direct them to join a different pair and introduce each other again, this time using a new piece of information. Repeat this process once or twice more so that the students have the opportunity to introduce their partners several times, while interacting with a number of other students in the class.

Have the students return to their seats and lead a brief discussion.

Discussion Questions:

1. What have you learned from this activity about how we are the same? ...about how we are different?
2. How does talking with and listening to others help you know them better?
3. Do you think that knowing another person well makes you less likely to have negative or bad feelings about that person? Why?
4. If you had a problem or conflict with someone, what could be gained by talking and listening to each other?

Topics:

One of my favorite T.V. shows is...
A time I felt afraid
One thing I value in a friend
A way I have fun is...
A game I enjoy playing
Something fun I did on summer vacation
I like it when somebody says to me...
Something I can do for myself is...

I get angry when...
I like people who...
Something I am learning right now
Something I do well is...
If I could have one wish it would be...
Something I really want to do
Something that makes me happy
Something that makes me sad
One thing that makes me a good friend is...

Understanding Prejudice
Discussion and Story-Writing

Objectives:

The students will:
— define the term *prejudice*.
— demonstrate understanding of the concept of prejudice.
— discuss how prejudice limits self and others.

Grades:

K-8

Procedure:

Read the following story to the class:

Once upon a time there was a boy named Tommy. Tommy was a nice boy who did well in school and had lots of friends. But Tommy had one peculiarity—he didn't like green peas. In fact, he really hated green peas. Although he had never eaten a green pea, he was sure if he did he would hate the taste. He wasn't exactly sure why he felt this way, he just knew that he did. Tommy wouldn't have anything to do with green peas; he just shut them out of his life and never had a good thing to say about them. As Tommy grew older his dislike for green peas grew and grew. One day he decided he didn't like green beans either, and then he didn't like lettuce. Pretty soon he disliked all green food, even pistachio ice cream! Since foods don't have any feelings, Tommy's negative attitude didn't hurt them. But Tommy sure missed out on a lot of good things!

After reading the story, write the word *prejudice* on the board and ask the students what the word means to them. Record all responses. As a class, select the most appropriate definition(s). Facilitate discussion by relating the prejudice (of Tommy in the story) toward green foods to prejudice toward people and groups of people.

Discussion Questions:

1. What was Tommy's reason for not liking green peas?
2. What do you think might happen if Tommy tried green peas and other green foods?
3. In what ways did Tommy miss out because of his prejudice against green foods?
4. How does ignorance (not getting to know someone or something) contribute to prejudice?
5. What are some ways that people show prejudice against others?
6. How do you think people feel when they experience prejudice from other people?

Extension:

Form small groups, and have each group create a role-play demonstrating one form of prejudice. Explain that the groups may either dramatize the effects of prejudice in real life or deal with fanciful themes, such as Tommy and the green peas. Have each group act out its play for the entire class.

What Do You See?

Art and Discussion

Objectives:

The students will:
— create individual graphic interpretations starting from the same set of lines.
— explain that differences in perception and interpretation result in part from each person's uniqueness.
— state that having different perceptions does not automatically make one person right and another wrong.

Grades:

1-8

Materials:

one copy of the experience sheet, "What Do You See?" for each student; art materials

Procedure:

Give each student a copy of the experience sheet, "What Do You See?". Ask the students to look at the lines for a few moments, allowing the lines to suggest a picture in their imagination.

Distribute the art materials. Direct the students to recall the picture in their imagination and draw it, incorporating the lines already on the page among the shapes and lines of their composition. Encourage independent work and discourage talking during this process. Assure the students that there is no right or wrong way to complete the assignment, but that you want each person to rely on his or her own creativity and imagination.

At the conclusion of the work period, go around the room and ask the students to share their pictures, describing how they perceived the pre-existing lines and how they incorporated them in their compositions. Facilitate a follow-up discussion, emphasizing differences in perception and interpretation.

Discussion Questions:

1. Were any of our pictures "right" or "wrong?"
2. If we all saw the lines differently, what other things in life do you think we might see differently?
3. What things do we see or interpret differently that could cause problems and conflicts?
4. Why is it important to understand that people have a right to see and interpret things in their own ways?
5. What can happen when people believe that their perceptions are the right ones and different perceptions are wrong?

What Do You See?

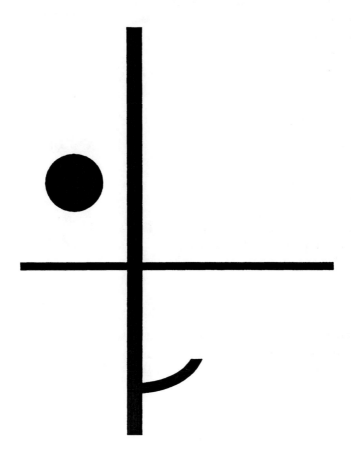

Listing Our Favorites

Objectives:

The students will:
— compare and demonstrate respect for each other's television preferences.
— state that people have different values and that values are neither right nor wrong.
— describe methods of showing respect for the values of others.

Grades:

1-8

Materials:

pencils, paper

Procedure:

Ask the students to take out paper and a pencil, and to write down their five favorite T.V. shows. Tell them to rank the shows, beginning with their very favorite at the top of the page. When they have finished, ask each student to read his or her list to the rest of the class. As the students share, occasionally note similarities and differences among their lists.

After all of the students have shared a list, facilitate a general discussion about individual preferences and how those relate to values. In the course of the discussion, attempt to arrive at a definition of the term *values*.

Discussion Questions:

1. Why isn't everyone's list the same?
2. If our lists are different, does that mean that some lists are better than others? Why or why not?
3. If your classmate's list is different from yours, is he or she wrong? Explain.
4. What causes us to like and dislike different things?
5. How can we learn to respect another person's values, even though they are different from ours?
6. What are some things we can do to show that we respect another person's opinions and values, even though we may not agree with them?

I Have a Friend Who Is Different From Me

A Sharing Circle

Objectives:

The students will:
— identify specific differences between themselves and their friends.
— demonstrate respect for differences in race, culture, lifestyle, attitude, and ability.

Grades:

K-8

Introducing the Topic:

Today we are going to talk about a friend who is different from us and what we like about that friend. The topic for this Sharing Circle is, "I Have a Friend Who Is Different From Me."

We are all alike in many ways, but we are also different. Today, I want you to think about a friend who is different from you in at least one way—and tell us why you like this person so much. Perhaps your friend is of a different race, or has a much larger family, or is many years older than you. Does your friend speak a different language or eat a different way than you do? Maybe your friend celebrates birthdays in a different manner than you do, or has different *holidays. What do you enjoy about this person? Does your friend listen to you and share things with you? Does he or she invite you to go places? Do you have something in common, like a love of sports, music, or computers? Think about it for a few minutes. The topic is, "I Have a Friend Who Is Different From Me."*

Discussion Questions:

1. What are some of the ways we differ from our friends?
2. Why do we like our friends even though they are different from us?
3. What causes people to dislike other people because of things like race or religion?

A Time I Felt Left Out

A Sharing Circle

Objectives:

The students will:
— identify a time when they were excluded or discriminated against.
— describe how all persons need to belong and feel accepted by others.

Grades:

K-8

Introduce the Topic:

The topic for this session is, "A Time I Felt Left Out." At one time or another, all of us have been left out of something that we wanted to be included in. Maybe you were left out of a game the other kids were playing because they thought you weren't good enough, or perhaps your family wouldn't let you participate in a project because they decided you were too young. Maybe you weren't feeling well and couldn't go to school on the day of a big field trip. Or maybe your friends were invited to a birthday party and you weren't. Perhaps you were excluded from an activity because you use a wheelchair, couldn't throw a ball, were overweight, or are black. Whatever the reason was, you felt left out of what others were doing. Think about it for a few moments. The topic is, "I Time I Felt Left Out."

Discussion Questions

1. How did most of us feel about being left out?
2. Why is it so important to feel included?
3. What could you have done to be included?
4. Why do people exclude others from their activities?
5. What can you do if you see that someone else is being left out?

Other Sharing Circle Topics

A Time I Accepted and Included Someone

Something About Me That's Special

Something I Enjoy Doing Because It Gives Me a Feeling of Accomplishment

A Time I Was Discriminated Against

A Way I'm Different From My Friends

Something About Me You Wouldn't Know Unless I Told You

I Was Rejected Because of Something I Couldn't Change

Understanding and Controlling Feelings

Children who have learned to understand, accept, and control their feelings are not only less vulnerable to conflict, they are better equipped to deal constructively with conflict when it occurs.

By the time we're adults, some of us are so afraid of losing or being wrong that any contradiction of our beliefs or threat to our "turf" triggers an explosion of negative emotion. Others of us—those who perhaps too often witnessed the destructive effects of someone else's rage—are so afraid of the strong negative emotions that we avoid conflict at all costs. We run away, repress our feelings, and deny our rights.

When we look at it logically, rationally, what is so bad about a disagreement? What is so surprising about the fact that two people have different perceptions of the same event, or different ideas about how something ought to be done? Every conflict is an opportunity to learn and to grow, but when conflict occurs, there isn't time to be logical. We react emotionally, instantly, and that's what's so scary.

Therapists' waiting rooms and attendance at 12-step meetings attest to the difficulty of unlearning emotional reactions once they are imbedded in our behavior patterns.

Before they can learn to express their feelings in ways that are not a threat to others or themselves, students need to understand and accept the full range of emotional reactions they experience. The activities in this section put particular emphasis on learning to deal with those emotions generally associated with conflict and are designed to help students:

- control negative emotions.
- understand the feelings of themselves and others.
- express their own feelings appropriately.
- associate damaging behaviors with the feelings they provoke.
- associate various events with feelings.
- understand anger and how to express it.
- recognize and accept feelings generated by conflict.

Literature Connections

The following list of children's literature is offered to augment the activities in this section. The books deal with a wide range of emotions and with the efforts of children to come to grips with their feelings. An effective approach would be to ask the students to read one or more of the books prior to beginning the activities. If your students are very young, read the books aloud in class. In both cases, generate discussion by asking open-ended questions designed to reinforce understanding of the concepts conveyed through the story.

Primary:

Holabird, Katherine, *Angelina's Birthday Surprise,* illustrated by Helen Craig, New York, Clarkson Potter, 1989.

Angelina, a young mouse, has an accident with her bicycle and ruins it. She tries to earn money for a new one, and is surprised by her friends with a bike for her birthday.

Viorst, Judith, *Alexander and the Terrible, Horrible, No Good, Very Bad Day*, illustrated by Ray Cruz, Atheneum, 1972.

This favorite tells about Alexander, who can tell that it is going to be a bad day when he wakes up with gum in his hair. When he gets out of bed he trips over his skateboard and, by mistake, drops his sweater in the sink while the water is running. Everything goes wrong all day, right down to the lima beans for supper and kissing on a T.V. show. Alexander's solution, to move to Australia, is finally reversed by an understanding mother.

Intermediate:

Jukes, Mavis, *Like Jake and Me*, illustrated by Lloyd Bloom, Knopf, 1984.

Cowboy Jake is his stepson's hero until he expresses terror at a wolf spider he finds in his clothing. His fear begins to make the boy and his stepfather feel closer to each other.

Carrick, Carol, *The Accident*, illustrated by Donald Carick, Clarion, 1976.

After his dog is accidentally hit by a truck and killed, Christopher must deal with his own feelings of depression, guilt, and anger. With the help of a caring father, he processes his grief.

Martin, Ann, *Stage Fright*, illustrated by Blanche Sims, Holiday House, 1984.

Learning that her 4th grade class is putting on a play terrifies Sara, who is painfully shy and depends upon her bouncy friend, Wendy. However, she does manage her few lines and learns that, with real effort, she can overcome her shyness someday.

Upper:

Paterson, Katherine, *Bridge to Terebithia,* illustrated by Donna Diamond, Thomas Y. Crowell, 1977.

Ten-year-old Jess becomes friends with Leslie, a newcomer to his fifth grade class, who starts off the school year by beating all the boys in their daily running races. When Leslie meets an untimely death trying to reach their hideaway in a storm, Jess has to cope with his feelings of guilt and grief.

O'Dell, Scott, *Island of the Blue Dolphins*, Houghton Mifflin, 1960.

In the early 1800's, an Indian girl spent 18 years alone on San Nicholas Island far off the coast of California. This novel is based on that story. It tells of Karana, who had to deal with the separation from her friends and family, the death of her father and younger brother, survival amid the dangers of wild dogs, storms, and even the Aleutian sea-otter hunters, plus extreme loneliness.

Things That "Bug" Us
Group List and Discussion

Objectives:

The students will:
— describe acceptable responses to things that upset them.
— explain why it is important to control negative behavior.

Grades:

2-8

Materials:

writing materials for students; chalkboard and chalk

Procedure:

Distribute writing materials, and ask the students to write down 10 things that really annoy them. Provide several examples, such as: *kids who butt in line, bullies on the playground, having too much homework, cigarette smoke, losing a game, getting a bad grade, being teased or laughed at, etc.*

Write the following headings in a single row across the top of the chalkboard: "Things That Bug Us!" "Our Feelings," and "How We Express Our Feelings."

When the students have finished their individual lists, ask several volunteers to each share one item. Write these on the board under the heading, "Things That Bug Us!" List about 10 items.

Go through the list, one item at a time. Ask the students to share some of the feelings they typically experience when confronted with each situation listed. Write these feelings in the second column. Then, go back through the list of feelings and ask the students to describe how they might express each one. Record their responses in the third column.

Finally, read across the chart and examine each row and item more closely. Ask the students to identify modes of expression that might be dangerous, get a person in trouble, and hurt others. Draw lines through these items. Ask the students to identify responses that are likely to have neutral or positive effects. Circle these items. Discuss why the circled items represent better ways of responding to annoying situations.

Discussion Questions:

1. What would happen if people never controlled their emotions and everyone expressed anger and frustration freely, with no thought about consequences? What would life be like?
2. How do people control their feelings? How do you control yours?
3. Would you rather have controls come from outside you or inside you? Why?

Extension:

Use this theme as the topic of a writing or art exercise: Have the students describe or draw a picture of a society in which people have no controls, internal or external, on their behavior.

How It Feels...
Creative Writing and Discussion

Objectives:

The students will:
— identify and describe their feelings in response to different experiences.
— describe behavioral choices available for responding to different experiences.
— describe how one person's behaviors affect the feelings of others.

Grades:

3-8

Materials:

writing materials for students; chalkboard and chalk or chart paper and markers

Procedure:

On the board or chart paper write the following list:

How it Feels...
...to be laughed at
...to be called names
...to be the last person chosen for a team
...to be included
...to be part of the crowd
...to get a bad grade
...to come in first
...to come in last

Explain to the students that you would like them to pick one topic and write a story that illustrates how a person might feel in that situation. Require that the students provide specific examples from their own experience, the experiences of others, or their imagination. Instruct them to describe the incident and the feelings of the individuals involved, but remind them not to use real names when describing actual experiences.

Discussion Questions:

Ask volunteers to read their stories to the class. Facilitate discussion after each reading, basing your questions on issues presented in the story. Conclude the activity by asking these and/or other general questions:
1. What good does it do to try to understand the feelings of others?
2. What thoughts did you have during this activity about how to treat other people?

Positive Communication
Discussion and Experience Sheet

Objectives:

The students will:
— state that feelings can be communicated either positively or negatively.
— describe appropriate ways of expressing feelings.
— explain how one's actions affect the feelings of others.

Grades:

2-8

Materials:

one copy of the experience sheet, "Communicating My Feelings," for each student

Procedure:

Write the heading, "Angry," on the chalkboard, and ask, "Who can tell me one way that you express yourself when you are angry?" Elicit several responses and, as succinctly as possible, record those responses in a column under the heading. Then ask, "Are these the best possible ways to respond when you're angry?"

Ask the students to brainstorm positive ways of handling anger. Accept all responses, but remind the students to keep their suggestions <u>positive</u>. Write these responses in a second column. When the second column is full, ask the following questions to facilitate discussion.

Discussion Questions:

1. How do you feel when you behave in the ways we listed in the first column?

2. Do these behaviors help you deal with your anger? Why or why not?

3. How do you think people around you feel when you express yourself in these ways?

4. How do you feel when you behave in the ways we listed in the second column?

5. Do these methods help you deal with your anger? Why or why not?

6. How do you think the people around you feel when you express yourself in these ways?

Pass out the experience sheet, "Communicating My Feelings," and go over the directions with the students. When the students have completed the experience sheet, ask volunteers to share their ideas concerning appropriate ways to express each feeling.

Communicating My Feelings

Everyone has feelings; they are a natural part of being human. We all share the same feelings, but we express those feelings in different ways. It is important for us to learn how to communicate our feelings appropriately.

Look at the feelings listed below. Describe in writing the things you do and say to express each feeling. Then see if you can think of *a better way* to express yourself, and write that down, too.

When I am angry, I usually express myself by: _____

_____

A *better* way to express my anger would be to: _____

_____

When I am sad, I usually express myself by: _____

_____

A *better* way to express my sadness would be to: _____

_____

When I am happy, I usually express myself by: _____

_____

A *better* way to express my happiness would be to: _____

_____

When I am discouraged, I usually express myself by: _____

_____

A *better* way to express my discouragement would be to: _____

_____

When I am scared, I usually express myself by: _____

_____

A *better* way to express my fear would be to: _____

_____

When I want attention I usually express myself by: _____

_____

A *better* way to receive attention would be to: _____

_____

Experience Sheet

Act Out a Feeling!
Dramatization and Discussion

Objectives:

The students will:
— identify feelings based on verbal and nonverbal cues.
— develop a working vocabulary of feeling words.
— state that feelings are natural and normal.
— describe the relationship between events and emotional reactions.

Grades

K-4

Materials:

one empty can, strips of paper, felt pen

Procedure:

Tell the students that you have observed them displaying a lot of different feelings today, just as they do every day. Then describe a specific incident in which you were able to discern a person's feelings clearly. For example, describe how one person was hurt by the criticism or name-calling of another person. (Don't identify the individuals involved.) Ask the children if they noticed other incidents involving feelings, both positive and negative. Without naming names, discuss the various emotions demonstrated by people they (and you) observed.

As the students name feelings, write each feeling word down on a paper strip and put it in the can. After you have deposited a number of strips in the can, ask, "How can you tell by looking at a person how he or she feels?" After several responses, announce that the students are going to have an opportunity to act out the feelings they've been discussing.

Ask volunteers to come to the front of the room, draw a strip of paper from the can, and act out the feeling written on the paper. Empha-size that the students may express the feeling in any way they wish, using both body and face, but *without naming* the feeling. Explain that the rest of the class will try to guess what the feeling is. Give all volunteers an opportunity to participate.

Discussion Questions:

Between dramatizations, facilitate discussion. Each time a new feeling is dramatized, ask the class these questions:
1. What might cause a person to feel this way?
2. Can you remember a time when you had this feeling? In just a few words, tell us what happened.

After each of the emotions has been dramatized several times, conclude the activity with these questions:
1. What did you learn about feelings today?
2. Does everyone have the feelings we acted out? How do you know?
3. When you feel one of these feelings, or some other feeling, is it okay?
4. When you feel angry or jealous, is it okay to do something that hurts another person? What can you do instead?

48

Feeling Faces
Identifying Feeling Sources

Objectives:

The students will:
— identify feelings based on facial expressions.
— describe situations that can lead to specific feelings.

Grades:

K-2

Materials:

"Animal Feeling Faces" duplicated on white construction paper (or tag board), tongue depressor or popsicle sticks, and glue

Procedure:

In advance, duplicate the six "Animal Feeling Faces" on white construction paper (or tagboard). Cut out each face and glue it to the end of a tongue depressor or stick, creating a mask with handle.

Gather 6 to 8 students into a circle and show them the "Animal Feeling Faces." Explain that each animal face expresses a feeling that everyone has at one time or another.

Announce that the students are going to play a feelings game. In your own words, explain: *I will hold up an animal face and name the feeling it shows. Raise your hand when you have thought of something that might cause that feeling. If I call on you, come up in front of the group, hold the animal feeling face, and tell us what you think could cause that feeling.*

Help each youngster describe a realistic situation that might cause the feeling depicted.

Continue until all of the feelings have been talked about.

In the second phase of the game, ask a volunteer to come forward and choose an "Animal Feeling Face." Ask him or her to name the feeling conveyed by the animal's expression, and describe a simple situation which might have caused that feeling. Help reluctant or shy students take a turn being "on stage." Again, do this until all six feeling faces have been used.

Ask volunteers to "perform" before the entire class. Have them choose a feeling face, name the feeling depicted, and describe a situation that might have caused the feeling.

Extension:

Keep the animal feeling faces on hand and use them when actual situations arise that result in real feelings. Ask the student involved in the situation to choose the "Animal Feeling Face" that tells how he or she feels. Then, ask the student to describe what caused the feeling.

Animal Feeling Faces

Surprised

Sad

Happy

Angry

Afraid

Shy

First Feelings
Experience Sheet and Discussion

Objectives:

The students will:
— learn and practice acceptable ways to express negative emotions.
— identify feelings that typically precede/ precipitate anger and identify ways to deal with them.

Grades:

4-8

Materials:

one copy of the experience sheet, "Dealing with Anger," for each student

Directions:

Write the heading, "Anger" on the chalkboard. Ask the class to brainstorm specific examples of angry behavior. List them beneath the heading. Then ask the students to describe how their bodies feel when they are angry, and talk briefly about the power of the emotion.

Read the following scenario to the class:

Desiree skipped out of her classroom happily. On her way home she boasted to her friend, Antonio, "All I have to do for homework is math, and it's a cinch. Math is my easiest subject. I always get A's." She ran into her house and threw down her backpack. Off she ran to play with friends until dinner. That evening she played games with her sister and watched some television, forgetting to do her homework. The next day in school, when her teacher asked for her Math homework, Desiree looked startled and then turned red. "I forgot to do it," she said, looking down at her backpack. As she looked up, Antonio was watching her from across the room. Desiree suddenly stuck her tongue out at him and wouldn't look at him for the rest of the morning. At recess she refused to play ball with Antonio and told him she was mad at him.

Following the story, facilitate discussion by asking these questions:
1. What were Desiree's first feelings when she realized that she had forgotten her homework?
2. How could she have expressed those feelings?
3. How did Desiree feel when she saw her friend Antonio watching her?
4. Why did she refuse to play with Antonio at recess?
5. How could Desiree have expressed her feelings toward Antonio?
6. What could she have done to control her behavior toward her friend?

Make the following points in a discussion about anger:
• Anger is a normal emotion. We all get angry and need to learn acceptable and effective ways to deal with anger.
• Anger tends to be a secondary feeling or emotion. In other words, one or more *other* feelings usually precede anger. For example, when Desiree realized she had forgotten to do her homework, her first emotions may have been shock, humiliation, panic, regret, and desperation in rapid succession.
• Another example: When a student fails a test for which she or he studied hard,

52

the first feelings are overwhelming disappointment and frustration. But anger follows so quickly that it's the only emotion the rest of the class observes. The same thing happens with other feelings, too.

- Other people usually have difficulty coping with someone's anger. This is partly because anger acts as a mask, hiding what is really going on. Others will have a much easier time responding to your frustration, grief, relief, sadness, or fear than to your anger. Consequently, a very valuable skill to develop is the skill of expressing your initial feelings, rather than just your anger.
- Anger puts stress on the body. Too much anger experienced too often can lead to illness.

Distribute the experience sheet, "Dealing with Anger." Go over the directions and give the students a few minutes to respond to the questions individually.

Have the students form small groups. Ask them to discuss the situations and their responses to the questions.

Discussion Questions:

1. What did you decide were Marco's first emotions? Jed's? Nieko's?
2. How could each character have expressed his or her first emotions?
3. What other behaviors did you come up with in each situation?
4. How does anger mask what is really going on?
5. Why is anger such a difficult emotion to deal with in other people?
6. If you have difficulty dealing with anger, what can you do to get help?

Extension:

Have volunteers role play several of the best alternatives suggested in each situation.

Dealing with Anger

Situation 1:

Marco and Jed were best buddies. After school, they often stayed on the playground to play their favorite game, basketball. During one game, as they were passing the ball back and forth, Marco suddenly spotted his dog running loose across the playground. "Here, Rambo," he shouted, as Jed slammed the ball his way. Marco felt the impact of the rapidly flying ball right on the side of his face, and fell to the ground. After rubbing his stinging face and catching his breath, Marco got up and started screaming at Jed. "Hey, you did that on purpose, you jerk." With tears streaming down his face, he ran toward his friend swinging his fists and shouting, "I am gonna get you back!" Backing away, Jed yelled, "It's your own fault, dummy. You weren't watching the ball!"

Questions:

What were Marco's first feelings after
he fell to the ground?

_____

_____

_____

_____

How did he express those feelings?

_____

_____

How could he have better expressed those feelings?

_____

_____

Situation 2:

Mieko had been attending gymnastics class in the evenings at the local gymnasium. She liked to do tumbling and easily performed handsprings, cartwheels, and flips. However, when it was her turn to work on the balance beam, Mieko didn't do all of the movements easily. One evening, Mieko was practicing turns on the beam and kept falling off. She just couldn't keep her balance. After practice, when Mieko's coach asked her to stay for a few minutes so he could give her some tips on how to keep her balance, she picked up her things and stormed out of the gym, slamming the door behind her. "He's just picking on me," Mieko grumbled as she stomped down the street.

Questions:

What were Mieko's first feelings when the coach asked her to stay after practice?

_____

_____

How did she express those feelings?

_____

_____

_____

How could she have better expressed
those feelings?

_____

_____

_____

_____

Something I Do That Makes Me Happy

A Sharing Circle

Objectives:

The students will:
— identify something that they enjoy doing.
— state that all people can make themselves feel better.

Grades:

K-8

Introduce the Topic:

Today we are going to think about things that we do to make ourselves feel good. The topic is, "Something I Do That Makes Me Happy."

Do you know that you can make yourself feel happy? We all do things every day to help ourselves feel good. We give hugs to people we love, and that feels good. We sometimes sing or dance or tell jokes to make ourselves happy. We might make ourselves happy by playing a favorite game or reading a good book; by getting together with a close friend, playing with a pet, relaxing in front of T.V., or taking a walk. Close your eyes right now and think of one thing that

you do to make yourself happy. Maybe you eat a favorite snack in the afternoon, or cuddle up with your cat. Perhaps you paint, or work on your computer. Take a few moments to think about it. The topic is, "Something I Do That Makes Me Happy."

Discussion Questions:

1. Why is it important to know how to make yourself feel better?

2. What ideas did you hear that you'd like to try?

3. Who is in control of how you feel? Explain.

How Conflict Makes Me Feel

A Sharing Circle

Objectives:

The students will:
— describe feelings they experience in conflict situations.
— identify ways to control their emotional reactions to conflict.

Grades:

K-8

Introduce the Topic:

Today we're going to talk about how we feel when we have a conflict with someone. The topic is, "How Conflict Makes Me Feel."

How do you feel inside when you are having an argument with your parent, or haven't spoken to your best friend for three days, or are fighting with someone over who is next in line? Maybe you get a shaky feeling, or your face gets hot, or you start to sweat. Perhaps you have trouble controlling your anger, or your tears. Some people say they feel powerful in a conflict, and others seem to feel weak. How do you usually feel? Take a few moments to think about conflicts *you've had, and tell us what usually happens to your emotions. The topic is, "How Conflict Makes Me Feel."*

Discussion Questions:

1. How did most of us seem to feel in conflict situations?
2. Why is it difficult to control our feelings in an argument?
3. What are some things you can do to feel more in control during a conflict?
4. How much of our bad feeling is caused by believing that conflict is bad? What can we do about that?

Additional Sharing Circle Topics

When I Like Myself Most

A Time I Felt Happy

A Time I Felt Sad

A Time I Felt Jealous

A Time I Couldn't Control My Feelings

A Time I Lost My Temper

A Time I Controlled My Temper

Something That Worries Me

Something That Makes Me Angry

An Ability I Have That I'm Proud Of

Something About My Culture That Makes Me Proud

Something About My Family That Makes Me Proud

Communicating Effectively

Good communication is a prerequisite to effective conflict resolution, and children who have learned to listen well and express themselves accurately are much better equipped in this arena. Effective communication *prevents* conflict among students by enabling them to understand each other at the outset. It *resolves* conflict by clarifying differences, goals, feelings, and needs.

Conflicts occur when people don't listen—or listen well enough. They also occur when people carelessly choose words that don't accurately represent their feelings and thoughts. We can't "give" each other our differing perceptions, so we explain ourselves with words. Words can bring us together and create understanding, or they can confuse us and create conflict.

With these basic tenants in mind, we've designed the activities in this section to help students:

- identify the ingredients of effective listening and speaking.
- understand and control nonverbal communication.
- learn the process of active listening.
- learn to use "I" messages to express their feelings and wishes in an assertive, but nonthreatening manner.
- experience the ability of precise language to prevent misunderstanding and conflict.
- learn to paraphrase as a method of seeking and offering clarification.
- experience the differences between assertive, aggressive, and passive behaviors and understand their effects in preventing and resolving conflict.

Literature Connections

The children's literature titles listed below all deal with one form or another of communication and are offered to augment the activities in this section. Ask the students to read one or more of the books prior to beginning the activities or throughout your implementation of them. If your students are very young, read the books aloud in class. In both cases, generate discussion by asking open-ended questions designed to reinforce understanding of the concepts conveyed through the story.

Primary:

Pinkwater, Manus, *The Bear's Picture,* illustrated by author, Dutton, 1984.

In this fable about truth and imagination, various people interpret and critique a little bear's painting, but his own interpretation is what makes the painting special.

Bunting, Eve, *The Valentine Bears,* illustrated by Jan Brett, Clarion, 1983.

Mrs. Bear plans a surprise Valentine's Day celebration for Mr. Bear despite their usual hibernating habits at that time of year. It is she who ends up delightfully surprised by her husband.

Intermediate:

White, E.B., *Charlotte's Web,* illustrated by Garth Williams, Harper & Row, 1952.

This beautiful story of loyalty and friendship begins when young Fern saves the life of a runt piglet named Wilbur. He later is also befriended by Charlotte, a lovely grey spider, who saves his life.

Cleary, Beverly, *Dear Mr. Henshaw,* illustrated by Paul O. Zelinsky, Morrow, 1983.

This Newberry Award book tells the story of a fourth grade boy, Leigh Botts, who aspires to be a writer when he grows up. He writes regularly to an author, and then writes in a journal about his parents' divorce, a move to a new school, and the daily disappearance of goodies from his lunch.

Upper:

Taylor, Theodore, *The Cay,* Doubleday, 1969.

After the Germans torpedoed the boat on which Phillip and his mother were travelling during World War II, Phillip found himself blind and stranded on a small Caribbean island with a black islander named Timothy. This is the story of their survival and of Phillip's efforts to understand the dignified, wise, and loving old man whom he had hated because of his race and culture.

Hamilton, Virginia, *Zeely,* illustrated by Symeon Shimin, Macmillan, 1967.

Eleven-year-old Geeder Perry finds a portrait of a Watutsi queen in an old magazine and decides that Zeely Tayber, who is six-and-a-half feet tall, thin, and deeply dark as ebony, must be a queen, too. Zeely helps bring Geeder back to reality and they become friends with much in common.

Communication Counts!
Sending and Receiving Messages

Objectives:

The students will:
— define communication and identify ways in which people communicate.
— state rules for effective listening and speaking.
— demonstrate good listening and speaking in a practice session.

Grades:

K-3

Materials:

chalkboard and chalk

Procedure:

Write the word *communication* on the chalkboard. Explain to the students that communication is a word that describes the way people send and receive messages. Ask the students to think of ways in which people communicate with each other. (talking face-to-face, telephone, writing, computer, television, radio, sign language, body language, etc.)

Ask two volunteers to come to the front of the class. Tell them to say something to each other. Point out that during verbal communication between two people, there is always a listener and a speaker. When one person speaks, the other listens. Usually both people take turns in both roles. Tell the students that good communicators know how to listen well, and they also know how to speak well. These are skills that anyone can learn.

Ask the students to help you generate a list of rules for good listening. Suggest that they think of someone who listens well to them, and describe the things that person does. Write their ideas on the chalkboard, making sure that the list includes these items:
- Look at the speaker.
- Think about, or picture, what the speaker is saying.

- Don't interrupt.
- Show the speaker that you are listening by nodding, smiling, or making brief comments like, "That's neat." or "Sounds like fun." or "That's too bad."
- If you don't understand something the speaker says, ask a question.

Now, ask the students to help you generate a list of rules for good speaking. Suggest that they think of someone they know who speaks well and describe what that person does. Write their ideas on the chalkboard, making sure that the list includes these items:
- Think about what you want to say before you speak.
- Speak clearly and loud enough to be heard, but don't shout.
- Share the time equally with the other person.
- Don't change the subject unless it's okay with the other person.

List some topics on the board that the students can use during a practice session. For example:
1. A school rule you appreciate and how it helps you.
2. A school rule you don't like, and how you'd change it.

3. The importance of complimenting others, and why it feels good to get a compliment.
4. Other methods of communicating that you use, such as writing and receiving letters.
5. Your pet and how you train and care for him/her.

Have the students pair up and sit together. Ask them to decide who is A and who is B. Announce that the A's will start the first conversation, using the topic of their choice. Tell the B's to join in the conversation, being a good listener at first, and a good speaker every time it is their turn to talk. Review the rules for both listening and speaking.

Allow the partners to talk for 3 to 5 minutes, depending on their level of interest. Then ask the B's to start a new conversation, using a different topic. Review the procedure and the rules as necessary. In a follow-up discussion, ask questions to encourage the students to talk about the experience:

Discussion Questions:

1. Which rules for good listening were easiest to follow? ...hardest to follow?
2. Which rules for good speaking were easiest to follow? ...hardest to follow?
3. Which rules, if any, don't you understand?
4. How did you feel when you were listening?
5. How did you feel when you were speaking?
6. How do you feel when someone listens well to you?
7. How can being a good listener help you in school? ...in your friendships? ...in your family?
8. How can being a good speaker help you?

Play Back!

A Preliminary Listening Exercise

Objectives:

The students will:
— demonstrate careful listening.
— describe the importance of good listening to friendships, family, and relationships.

Grades:

K-8

Materials:

audiocassette recorder and blank tape

Procedure:

Preparation: While the students are working, inconspicuously move around the room and tape some of their comments and casual conversation. Try to get clear recordings of individual student's voices that will be easily recognized.

Begin playing the recorded sounds at a relatively low volume, and then gather the students together. Write "Listen!" on the chalkboard in large letters. Point to the word and use other nonverbal signals to get the students to obey the written command. Let them listen to the sound of the tape recorder for a few moments, and then turn it off. Ask the students what they think they heard. Accept their responses, and then suggest that the tape recorder was "listening" to them while they worked. Ask the students, "What is special about the way a tape recorder listens?"

Facilitate responses to the question, helping the students recognize that a tape recorder is usually very accurate. If it is working properly, a tape recorder hears every word just the way it is said. In your own words say to the students: *You and a partner are going to take turns pretending to be tape recorders. When you are a tape recorder, you must listen very carefully to every word your partner says. Then, when your partner asks you to "play back" your recording, you will be able to repeat—just like a tape recorder—the things your partner told you.*

Have the students choose partners. Ask them to decide who will play the part of the tape recorder first. Have the "tape recorders" raise their hands. Explain that the other students will talk first, and that you will call time after one minute. Announce this topic:

"What I'm Going To Do After School Today"

Tell the speakers to start talking and the "tape recorders" to start recording. Call time after 1 minute. Give the next instruction: *Now the "tape recorders" will have 1 minute to repeat what they heard, while the speakers listen.*

Call time after 1 minute and ask the students these questions:
— What was it like to listen like a tape recorder?
— Speakers, how well did your tape recorder work?
— What was it like to be listened to so well?

Have the students switch roles and repeat the entire process, using the same topic. Then, ask the students to find new partners. Lead another round of the activity (with both partners having a turn) using this topic:

"What I'd Like To Do on My Birthday"

As time and interest permit, conduct additional rounds, switching partners and topics with each new round. Lead a follow-up discussion, focusing on the importance of listening.

Discussion Questions:

1. Why is it important to listen carefully when someone is talking?
2. How do you feel when someone listens to you and tries to understand everything you say?
3. How do you feel when the person you are talking to doesn't listen?
4. Why is it important to listen to your parents? ...your teacher? ...your friends?
5. Can good listening help people solve problems and conflicts that they have with each other? How?

Actions Speak Loudly!

Identifying Nonverbal Signals

Objectives:

The students will:
— correctly identify feelings based on nonverbal behaviors.
— explain how nonverbal communication works, and how it is related to listening and conflict resolution.

Grades:

1-8

Materials:

several 3-inch by 5-inch cards, each with one of the following feeling words written on it: *surprised, ashamed, disgusted, scared, excited, bored, sad, frustrated, angry, happy*

Procedure:

Begin by involving the students in a general discussion concerning the communication process. Explain that people usually communicate with each other by sending and receiving words. Words are like a *code* for thoughts and feelings. Another very important part of communication is the sending and receiving of nonverbal *signals*. Even when no words are spoken, people convey their thoughts and feelings through facial expression, posture, hand gestures, and other body movements. Part of being a good communicator is developing the ability to understand what these nonverbal signals mean.

Ask the students to think of some ways in which they communicate without words. When a volunteer responds, ask him/her to act out the response in front of the group.

Ask the students to form a large circle (two concentric circles if the class is very large), and randomly distribute the feeling-cards. Announce that the class is going to play a game in which different students act out the feelings written on the cards. Explain: *One at a time, each of you who has a card will come to the middle of the circle and nonverbally act out the feeling on your card. Remember, you may not use words. The rest of us will try to figure out what emotion you are dramatizing.*

If you have time after one complete round of dramatizations, redistribute the cards to new students and repeat the process. If you like, incorporate additional feeling words in the mix. Facilitate a follow-up discussion.

Discussion Questions:

1. How did you figure out the feelings?
2. Why is it important to understand the feelings of others?
3. Why do people express their feelings in different ways?
4. If you're not sure what someone is feeling, how can you find out?
5. When people communicate one feeling with words and a totally different feeling with nonverbal signals, which do you think is the person's real feeling? Why?
6. How can being aware of nonverbal communication help you avoid conflicts with others? ...resolve conflicts with others?

Note: If your students are very young, instead of writing the feeling words on cards, whisper them to individual students, and have those students act out the feelings in front of the group.

The Active Receiver
Communication Skill Practice

Objectives:

The students will:
— define the role of the receiver in communication.
— identify and demonstrate "active listening" behaviors.

Grades:

4-8

Materials:

a diagrammatic model of the communications process (see directions, below) drawn on the chalkboard or chart paper; a list of topics written on the chalkboard (see next page)

Procedure:

On the chalkboard and chart paper, draw a simple diagram illustrating the communication process. For example, print the words, **SENDER** and **RECEIVER** and draw two arrows—one going in each direction—between the two words. Explain to the students that in order for two people to enjoy and encourage each other, to work, play, or solve problems together, they need to be able to communicate effectively. In your own words, say: *In every example of communication, no matter how small, a message is sent from one person (the sender) to the other person (the receiver). The message is supposed to tell the receiver something about the feelings and/or thoughts of the sender. Because the sender cannot "give" the receiver his or her feelings and thoughts, they have to be "coded" in words. Good communicators pick words that describe their feelings and thoughts as closely as possible. Nonverbal "signals" almost always accompany the verbal message; for example, a smile, a frown, or a hand gesture. Sometimes the entire message is nonverbal. Good communicators send nonverbal signals that exactly match their feelings and thoughts.*

Ask the students to describe what a good receiver says and does to show that he or she is interested in what the sender is saying and is really listening. Write their ideas on the chalkboard. Be sure to include these behaviors:
1. Face the sender.
2. Look into the sender's eyes.
3. Be relaxed, but attentive.
4. Listen to the words and try to picture in your own mind what the sender is telling you.
5. Don't interrupt or fidget. When it is your turn to respond, don't change the subject or start telling your own story.
6. If you don't understand something, wait for the sender to pause and then ask, "What do you mean by..."
7. Try to feel what the sender is feeling (show empathy).
8. Respond in ways that let the sender know that you are listening and understand what is being said. Ways of responding might include nodding, saying "uh huh," or giving feedback that proves you are listening, for example:

- Briefly summarize: "You're saying that you might have to quit the team in order to have time for a paper route."
- Restate feelings: "You must be feeling pretty bad." or "You sound really happy!"

Tell the students that this type of listening is called *active listening*. Ask them if they can explain why the word *active* is used to describe it.

Ask the students to form groups of three. Tell them to decide who is **A**, who is **B**, and who is **C**. Announce that you are going to give the students an opportunity to practice active listening. Explain the process: *In the first round, **A** will be the sender and **B** will be the receiver and will use active listening. **C** will be the observer. **C's** job is to notice how well **B** listens, and report his/her observations at the end of the round. I will be the timekeeper. We will have three rounds, so that you can each have a turn in all three roles. When you are the sender, pick a topic from the list on the board, and remember to pause occasionally so that your partner can respond.*

Signal the start of the first round. Call time after 3 minutes. Have the observers give feedback for 1 minute. Tell the students to switch roles. Conduct two more rounds. Lead a follow-up discussion.

Discussion Questions:

1. How did it feel to "active listen?"
2. What was it like to be the observer?
3. When you were the sender, how did you feel having someone really listen to you?
4. What was easiest about active listening? What was hardest?
5. What did you learn from your observer?
6. Why is it important to learn to be a good listener?
7. When you have a conflict with someone, how can active listening help?

List of topics:

"A Time I Needed Some Help"
"Something I'd Like to Do Better"
"A Problem I Need to Solve"
"A Time I Got Into an Argument"
"A Time I Had to Make a Tough Decision"
"Something I'd Like to Be or Do When I'm an Adult"

Don't Say "You," Say "I"

Experience Sheet and Discussion

Objectives:

The students will:
— compare "I" messages and "you" messages and describe their differences.
— identify the three parts of an "I" message.
— practice formulating "I" messages.

Grades:

4-8

Materials:

one copy of the experience sheet, "Don't Say 'You'—Say 'I'" for each student; chalkboard and chalk or chart paper and magic marker; diagram of the communications model (see the activity, "The Active Receiver") on the board or chart

Procedure:

Review the communications model used in the activity, "The Active Receiver." Ask the students to summarize the roles of the sender and receiver. Then in your own words, explain to the students: *When you are the sender, one of the most powerful messages you can send— especially if you are having a problem or conflict with the receiver is an "I" message. An "I" message tells the receiver what the problem is, how you feel about it, and what you want (or don't want) the receiver to do. Many times, we send "you" messages when we would be much better off sending "I" messages. "You" messages are often blaming and threatening, frequently make the receiver feel mad or hurt, usually make the problem worse, and many times don't even describe the problem. "You" messages can even* start *a conflict where none existed before.*

Extemporaneously demonstrate with one or two of your students. For example, say:

Rodney, you are fooling around again. If you don't get busy and finish that assignment, the whole group will have to stay in during recess, and it will be your fault!
   vs.
Rodney, I'm worried that this assignment won't be finished by recess and the group will have to stay in. I'd like to see you concentrate much harder on your work.

Anna, are you forgetful or just lazy? Look at all those open marking pens. You ruined them!
   vs.
Anna, I get very discouraged when I see that the marking pens have been left open all night, because they dry out, and then we can't use them anymore. I want you to help me by remembering to cover them.

Distribute the experience sheets. Go over the directions with the students. Allow a few minutes for the students to individually complete the experience sheet.

When the students have completed their experience sheets, conduct brief role plays of

68

each cartoon. Take one cartoon at a time, and ask two volunteers to demonstrate first the "you" message, and then their own "I" messages. Invite other members of the class to come forward, step into the role play, and substitute their own "I" message. Contrast the various efforts and discuss their effectiveness.

Discussion Questions:

1. What is the hardest part of composing an "I" message?
2. How do you feel when someone gives you a "you" message? ...an "I" message?
3. How can using "I" messages help us settle arguments and resolve conflicts?

Don't Say "You"—Say "I"

Good Communication is the Key!

When another person does something we don't like, we may be tempted to send the person a **"you" message**. "You" messages get their name from the fact that they often start with the word "you." They are blaming messages. They can make the other person feel mad or hurt—and they can make the situation worse.

Try using an **"I" message** instead. "I" messages talk about your feelings and needs. They can help the other person understand you. Here's how to make an "I" message:

1. **Describe the situation.** It may help to begin with the words, "When..." or "When you..."
2. **Say how you feel.** "When you......................., I feel.............................."
3. **Describe what you want the person to do.** "When you................, I feel..............., and I want you to....................................."

Now, you try it! Read the "you" message in the first cartoon bubble. Then write a better message—an "I" message—in the second bubble.

REMEMBER— Use "I" Messages in Real Life!

Experience Sheet

Language as Pilot
A Communications Experiment

Objectives:

The students will:
— practice communicating clearly and accurately.
— describe problems caused by imprecise communication and differing interpretations.

Grades:

3-8

Materials:

desks, tables, crumpled paper, and other objects generally available in the classroom

Procedure:

Begin by telling the students that you would like them to cooperate in conducting an experiment that relates to language and communication. Without any further explanation, ask the students to help you build a runway. Construct the runway out of furniture and people. Make it about 15 to 20 feet long and wide enough for a person to walk down. Next, litter the runway with debris, books, papers, pencils, and other small objects which will not cause a blindfolded person to trip or fall.

When the runway is ready, ask a student volunteer to role play the pilot of an airplane landing on the runway. Then ask a volunteer to play the part of the air-traffic controller trying to help the pilot land the plane by giving directions over an imaginary radio transmitter. As soon as two students volunteer, ask them to move to opposite ends of the runway.

Blindfold the pilot. Explain that a storm has hit and lightning has knocked out the transmitter of the plane. The receiver is still working so the pilot can get messages, but can't send them. Indicate that the storm has created havoc on the runway. Debris is all over the place. The control tower must try to land the plane without damage by sending directions

over the radio. The visibility is zero, so the pilot must rely only on these messages for a safe landing. If the pilot brushes against any of the objects on the runway, the plane is considered crashed.

Allow several teams of pilots and controllers to attempt to land the plane safely. After each attempt, briefly discuss the problems each team encountered.

Ask the students to put the classroom back in order and return to their seats for a general discussion.

Discussion Questions:

1. How did you feel when you were the pilot?
2. How did you feel when you were the controller?
3. How can we communicate clear and exact messages?
4. Has anything like this ever happened to you? Tell us about a time when you had trouble getting a precise message across or correctly understanding someone else's message.
5. What have you learned about language and communication from this experiment?

The Choice Is Yours!

Experience Sheet and Group Experiment

Objectives:

The students will:
— demonstrate the skills of paraphrasing and summarizing.
— explain how paraphrasing and summarizing improve listening skills.
— explain how paraphrasing can aid in conflict resolution.

Grades:

5-8

Materials:

one copy of experience sheet, "The Choice Is Yours!" for each student

---

Procedure:

Ask the students to help you review the skill of *active listening* (See the activity, "The Active Receiver.") Jot notes on the board, reminding the students that active listening enables the listener not only to hear the words of the speaker, but to understand the speaker's feelings. Active listening encourages the speaker to explore his or her thoughts more deeply, and conveys a spirit of understanding and concern.

Point out that even when a person is listening, it is not uncommon to incorrectly hear or to misinterpret what is being said. One way to avoid misunderstanding is to give *feedback* to the speaker from time to time, summarizing or paraphrasing the main points of his or her statements. It is not necessary to repeat every word the speaker says, only the main points.

Demonstrate by asking a volunteer to paraphrase what you just said. Suggest that the student begin his or her feedback with the words, "You said..." or "You're saying...."

Announce that the students are going to have an opportunity to practice summarizing

and paraphrasing. Distribute the experience sheet and read through the "Situation" and the "Directions" with the class. Explain that this exercise has only two rules: First, during the discussion, everyone has an opportunity to speak. Second, before a person speaks, he or she must paraphrase or summarize what the last speaker said *to that speaker's satisfaction.*

Ask the students to form groups of five or six. Announce that it is the responsibility of all members of the group to monitor the discussion and enforce the paraphrasing rule.

At the conclusion of the exercise, ask the groups to report to the class. Facilitate a discussion about communication in general and paraphrasing in particular.

Discussion Questions:

1. How did you feel when your contributions were paraphrased?
2. How did you feel when you were doing the paraphrasing?
4. Does paraphrasing make communication easier or harder? Explain.
5. How can paraphrasing help you settle arguments and resolve conflicts?

The Choice Is Yours!

Situation:

Your class just won the national Junior Astronaut contest. The students may choose one of five prizes, each worth approximately $5000. Your committee's job is to decide which prize to recommend to the rest of the class. The students have only three days to accept a prize. If they cannot agree by the deadline, the prize will be awarded to the first runner-up.

Directions:

Your committee will have 15 minutes to reach consensus (agree) on one recommendation. You may *not* decide by a majority vote.

Choices:

1. The entire class will take a three-day trip to a nearby training facility for astronauts.
2. The class will choose two representatives who, along with their teacher, will travel to Houston, Texas, as special guests of NASA for the launching of the next manned space mission.
3. The class will receive a new computer system with communications software enabling students to network with junior astronauts at other schools throughout the country.
4. The class will donate the money to a research organization attempting to find solutions to environmental problems. In return, a plaque engraved with every student's name will be permanently displayed in the lobby of the research building.
5. Each student in the class will receive approximately $165 to use any way s/he chooses.

Feel the Difference
Assertiveness Practice

Objectives:

The students will:
— nonverbally demonstrate three response styles: passive, aggressive, and assertive.
— describe feelings and consequences associated with the three response styles.
— practice responding assertively in specific situations.

Grades:

K-4

Materials:

one copy of the response situations (next page) and one of the experience sheet "What's Your Behavior Style?" for each student

Procedure:

On the chalkboard, write the following pairs of response roles:

Passive Polly
Wimpy Walter

Demanding David
Aggressive Anna

Assertive Sean
Confident Connie

Distribute the experience sheets. If you teach non-readers, paraphrase the descriptions on the sheet while the students look at the illustrations. Have older students read through the experience sheet themselves.

Talk to the students about the differences between passive, aggressive, and assertive behaviors. Ask them which behavior style they usually use.

Ask two volunteers (a girl and a boy) to come to the front of the class and demonstrate the nonverbal attitudes and behaviors they would expect each pair of listed characters to exhibit. Get the class involved by asking: *What kind of facial expression would a Passive Polly have? How would Wimpy Walter stand? What are some gestures Demanding David might use? What kind of posture does Assertive Sean have?* Etc.

Ask the students to form groups of three. Have the members of each group divide the three response roles (passive, aggressive, and assertive) between them. Give each group a copy of the response situations described below.

Have the groups role-play each situation three times, with each member of the group responding according to his or her role. Instruct them to switch response roles between situations, so that every member has a chance to practice all three response styles. When it is not their turn to respond to a situation, group members are to play the other roles in the scenario or act as "drama coach," to the responder. Encourage the students to get in touch with their feelings in each role, and to dramatically demonstrate the differences between the three styles.

After the students have completed the role plays, lead a culminating discussion.

Discussion Questions:

1. How did you feel when you were being passive? ...aggressive? ...assertive?
2. How did you feel when you were responded to passively? ...aggressively? ...assertively?
3. Why is assertive behavior less threatening to the other person than aggressive behavior?
4. What would happen if you were always passive? ...always aggressive?
5. How can a shy person learn to be more assertive? ...an aggressive person?

Extension:

Have the students write a 1-page story about one of the response roles (Passive Polly, Assertive Sean, etc.). Tell them to describe a situation (or use one of the situations listed here), how their character responds in the situation, and what happens as a result.

Response Situations

1. You and your friend plan to go to the movies this weekend, but you can't agree on what movie to see. Your friend picked the movie last time, so you think it's your turn to choose. However, your friend is resisting because his or her parent already saw the movie you've chosen and didn't like it.

2. You are standing in a long cafeteria line, waiting to order your lunch and a drink. Just as your turn comes up, another student cuts in, saying thathe or she is in a big hurry and can't wait. When you object, the student first pleads, then starts to get angry, calling you names.

3. You and your brother (sister) share a room. Your parent has threatened to ground you both for the weekend if the room isn't cleaned up before supper today. You always keep your things neat, and think that your brother should do the cleaning, since it's his mess. Your brother says he won't do anything unless you help.

What"s Your Behavior Style

Passive Polly rarely stands up for her own rights. She does whatever other people want her to do, even if it's wrong. Like **Wimpy Walter**, she slumps and slouches, and doesn't look people in the eye when she talks to them.

Demanding David is just like **Agressive Anna**. They don't care about the feelings or rights of others. They just want to get their own way, even if they have to put other people down in the process. Aggressive Anna is often loud and sarcastic. Demanding David frequently gets into fights with other kids.

Assertive Sean and **Confident Connie** know how to stand up for their own rights and, at the same time, respect the rights of others. They don't let people talk them into doing things that are bad for them, and they take responsibility for their own actions. You can tell they feel good about themselves by the way they stand up straight and speak up clearly.

Experience Sheet

What's Your Style?
Creative Dramatics

Objectives:

The students will:
— demonstrate assertive, aggressive, and passive response styles.
— explain why assertiveness is the most effective and positive of the response styles.

Grades:

5-8

Materials:

one copy of the experience sheet, "Reacting Assertively" for each student

Procedure:

Write the words "Passive," "Aggressive," and "Assertive" on the board. Explain to the students that these labels represent styles of responding to people and events. Two of the styles tend to create problems. The third style is usually very effective. Using the following information, explain the styles, giving an example of each.

• *Aggressive*

An aggressive person acts like a bully and pushes others around—physically, verbally, or both. He or she responds to situations by speaking loudly, acting or sounding angry, and using threats, accusations, and name-calling. An aggressive person doesn't respect the rights of others, and can make you feel angry, hurt, or scared.

• *Passive*

A passive person is what you might call "wishy-washy." He or she speaks very softly, slumps, doesn't look at you, and may even appear scared or nervous. Passive people feel unsure. They usually let others make the decisions, and then go along with those decisions—even when they are dangerous or wrong.

• *Assertive*

If you usually stand up for what you want, while respecting the rights of others, you probably have an assertive response style. You look directly at others without staring in a threatening way, and speak up confidently, without yelling. You don't always do what the crowd does. You follow through on your responsibilities to other people.

Read the situations below, and ask volunteers to demonstrate how a person might respond using each of the three response styles:

1. The class is on the basketball court, and is choosing teams for a game. You want to play center, but so do two other students.

2. You are at a birthday party. The kids start talking about playing a trick on a friend of yours who is not there.

3. Two friends come to your house one Saturday and ask if they can come in. Your parents left for the day, and said you may not have company. You want to obey your parents, but your friends

make it hard for you. They insist that no one will know.

Distribute the experience sheets and go over the instructions. Allow the students time to complete the sheets individually, then ask them to form groups of four or five. Direct the groups to dramatize the three situations described on the experience sheet, taking turns playing the aggressive, passive, and assertive roles. Circulate and assist. If time permits, ask some of the groups to repeat their dramatizations for the entire class.

Lead a summary discussion. Ask the students to think about the three response styles and answer these questions:

Discussion Questions:

1. What are the main differences between the response styles?
2. Which response style is the most effective? Why?
3. How can a passive person become more assertive?
4. How can an aggressive person become more assertive?

Reacting Assertively

Read these situations and decide which response is **aggressive**, which is **passive**, and which is **assertive**. After each response circle your choice. When you have finished, get together with your group and act out the situations.

Situation 1:

You and some friends are having a conversation outside a convenience store after school. A police officer approaches and begins questioning you about your activities.

Responses:

- You step back and let one of your friends do all the talking. (aggressive, passive, assertive)
- You stand up straight and speak up clearly, answering all of the officers questions in a businesslike way. (aggressive, passive, assertive)
- You roll you eyes at your friends, become defensive, and demand to know what the officer thinks you're doing. (aggressive, passive, assertive)

Situation 2

A few weeks ago, your parent outlined some chores for you to do around the house and yard on a regular basis. You are getting behind in those chores because of activities at school and with your friends. Your parent threatens to ground you if you don't catch up on your chores within the next couple of days.

Responses:

- You apologize, explaining that you too have been concerned about the chores because of a recent increase in your other activities. You ask your parent to help you work out a schedule that better utilizes your time. (aggressive, passive, assertive)
- You listen sullenly, then go in your room and cry, all the while telling yourself that your parent is mean and is deliberately making life miserable for you. (aggressive, passive, assertive)
- You get angry and tell your parent he or she is being unfair, go outside, slamming the door behind you and start banging tools around as you work in the yard. (aggressive, passive, assertive)

Situation 3

You and two other students are working as a team on a computer project. You start to argue concerning what step should come next, and in the process raise your voices and begin gesturing and pushing each other around in a friendly way. Your teacher breaks up the argument, sends you to your desks, and tells you that you will have to finish the assignment separately.

Responses:

- You shrug your shoulders, go to your desk, and spend the rest of the period sullenly doodling in the margin of your book. (aggressive, passive, assertive)
- You wait until the teacher is finished talking, then state that you would like to explain what happened. You acknowledge that you were loud and may have disrupted the class and promise to be more careful when you have disagreements in the future. You say that, in your opinion, all members of the team will do a better job on the assignment and learn more if allowed to continue working together. (aggressive, passive, assertive)
- You complain loudly that the teacher isn't being fair because you were only having a normal disagreement. You tell the teacher that if you can't finish the project it won't be your fault, and make a face when he or she turns away. (aggressive, passive, assertive)

Practice being assertive!

Respect the rights of others and stand up for your own.

Experience Sheet

A Time I Really Felt Heard

A Sharing Circle

Objectives:

The students will:
— describe the importance of listening to others.
— describe feelings generated by being recognized and heard.

Grades:

K-8

Introduce the Topic:

Today our topic is, "A Time I Really Felt Heard." We know that attention is a universal need. Sometimes we do not get attention for one reason or another, but when we do our feelings are usually positive.

Think of a time when you really needed to be heard and someone listened to you. Perhaps you had some kind of problem that you wanted to solve, or maybe you had an experience that you wanted to tell someone about. Who listened to you? How did you feel after you had expressed yourself? Think about it for a few moments. The topic is, "A Time When I Really Felt Heard."

Discussion Questions:

1. How do we usually feel when our feelings are not accepted?
2. Do you ever keep your feelings to yourself because you think no one is interested?
3. When people risk saying how they feel, do you respect them for it? Why or why not?
4. How did you feel about the person who listened to you?
5. What happens in a conversation when people don't listen to each other?

How I Let Others Know I'm Interested In What They Say

A Sharing Circle

Objectives:

The students will:
— identify specific behaviors that convey their interest as a listener.
— describe the importance of good listening.

Grades:

K-8

Introduce the Topic:

Our topic for this session is, "How I Let Others Know I'm Interested in What They Say." One way we can let another person know that we are listening and interested in what they have to say is by what we say in response. There are many other things we can do, too. Some of these involve our posture, the way we make eye contact, or whether and how frequently we interrupt them. Think of some of the ways you show other people that you are interested in what they are saying. Also think about how you feel when others listen to you with interest. Select one of the ways that you show interest and tell us about it. Our topic is, "How I Let Others Know I'm Interested In What They Say."

Discussion Questions:

1. How do you think people feel knowing that you are really interested in what they have to say?
2. How do you feel knowing that others are interested in what you have to say?
3. What can you do to become a more effective listener and communicator?
4. Why is good listening so important?

Additional Sharing Circles

What I Think Good Communication Is

A Time When I Accepted Someone Else's Feelings

A Time I Listened Well To Someone

Once When Someone Wouldn't Listen to Me

How I Got Someone to Pay Attention to Me

Someone I Know Who Is a Good Speaker

A Time I Expressed Myself Well

A Time I Had Trouble Expressing Myself

A Time I Was at a Loss for Words

A Time I Was Misunderstood

A Time When Poor Communication Caused a Fight

We Solved the Problem by Listening to Each Other

Cooperation and Teambuilding

Groups outside of the world of sports that have developed a degree of cooperation and collaboration sufficient to have earned them the title of *team* are a relative rarity, but are certainly worth emulating. To have it said that your class is a true team is an accolade of the highest order. Teams function through interdependence and inclusion. Members are valued for their uniquenesses; they trust one another and turn to each other for help and advice. Teams subdivide easily and demonstrate remarkable creativity and problem-solving ability.

Teams are not without conflict, but when they experience conflict, they have the motivation and the means to find resolutions in which every member wins. They have learned, usually through the long and arduous process of becoming a team, that if one person loses, everyone loses.

Teambuilding activities have been a staple of organizational development for decades, and have recently found wide acceptance in schools through the immensely popular and successful cooperative-learning movement. The activities in this section, many based on classic organizational development approaches, are designed to help students:

- identify the ingredients of cooperative relationships.
- identify the advantages of working cooperatively with others.
- assess their behavior in group situations.
- appreciate the viewpoints and values of others.
- develop accountability and trust.
- identify ways they can count on one another.
- distinguish between cooperative and competitive behaviors.
- recognize how cooperative behaviors facilitate goal attainment and prevent conflict.
- practice cooperative, supportive, and collaborative behaviors in completing specific tasks.

Literature Connections

Use some of these selections from children's literature to set the stage for teambuilding activities. Read them to younger students. Require older students to read them on their own. In both cases, follow up with discussion questions to reinforce learning and stimulate higher-level thinking.

Primary:

de Paola, Tomie, *Now One Foot, Now the Other*, Putnam, 1981.

This story explores the relationship between a child and his grandfather. When Bobby is a baby, grandfather Bob helps him learn to walk. Years later when grandfather has a stroke, young Bobby helps him learn to walk again.

Havill, Juanita, *Jamaica Tag-Along,* illustrated by Anne Sibley O'Brien, Houghton Mifflin, 1989.

Jamaica likes to follow her big brother, who doesn't appreciate having her around when he plays serious baseball. She learns how he feels when a younger child wants to help her build a sand castle. In the end they all help each other.

Hall, Donald, *Ox-Cart Man*, illustrated by Barbara Cooney, Viking Press, 1979.

In early New England, a man packs his goods in the ox-cart to sell at Portsmouth Market, where he can buy provisions for his family. The whole family contributes to the goods: a shawl his wife made, mittens his daughter knitted, linen the women wove, birch brooms his son made, and even wool from the sheep and a bag of feathers from the goose.

Intermediate:

McKissack, Patricia, *Nettie Jo's Friends*, illustrated by Scott Cook, New York, Knopf, 1989.

Nettie Jo wants to take her doll to a wedding, but the doll must have a new dress to be presentable. As all of the needles in the family are being used, she sets out to find one. In her search, she aids a rabbit, a fox, and a panther, who in turn come to her rescue.

Pasternak, Carol, and Allen Sutterfield, *Stone Soup,* illustrated by Hedy Campbell, Women's Press (Canada), 1974/1980.

Susan brings an unusual rock to school, and Mr. O'Leary, the janitor, invites the class to the basement to make stone soup with it. The multi-ethnic children help make the soup using yams, badams, and other exotic foods. They learn each other's cultural dances as well.

Upper:

Anacona, George, *Riverkeeper,* Macmillan, 1990.

A group of concerned citizens living along the Hudson River organize and hire John Cronin to work as a riverkeeper to track down polluters and bring them to court. Because of their efforts, and his, they help to restore the beauty and safely of the Hudson.

Geroge, Jean Craighead, *The Missing 'Gator of Gumbo Limbo,* Harper Collins, 1992.

Liza K. and her mother leave home to escape an abusive father and find shelter in Gumbo Hammock in the Florida Everglades. They are befriended by a naturalist, a homeless poet, and a would-be singer who all work together to save the local alligator and the environment of the hammock.

Working Together
Discussion and Experience Sheet

Objectives:

The students will:
— define the word *cooperate*.
— describe the benefits of cooperating with others to achieve a goal.

Grades:

1-4

Materials:

one copy of the experience sheet, "Together Is Better" for each student; chalkboard and chalk

Procedure:

Write the word *cooperate* on the board. Ask the students what it means to cooperate with another person. Accept all contributions, jotting key words and phrases on the board. Attempt to agree upon a simple definition of the word.

Remind the students of specific occasions when you have asked groups of two or more to work together to complete a task or assignment. Ask them to think carefully about what they accomplished and how they went about it. Then ask, "What did you gain by working together cooperatively?"

Again, accept all contributions. Through questions and discussion, help the students identify the following potential benefits of working cooperatively with another person:

- When people work together, they save time.
- When people work together, they think of more solutions to a problem.

- When people work together, their solutions are more creative.
- When people work together, they have fun.
- When people work together, they do a better job.

Distribute the experience sheets. After going over the directions, give the students a few minutes to complete the sheet. If time permits, have the students share what they have written in small groups. Facilitate a culminating class discussion.

Discussion Questions:

1. What are some ways that you cooperate with others at home?
2. Why is it important to cooperate when working with others?
3. What happens when one person in a group is uncooperative?
4. If you had an uncooperative person in your group, what could you do?

Together Is Better

In the space below, write two or three sentences that describe what **cooperating** means to you. Below are some words that you might want to use. Use other words, too.

share	team	together	listen	talk
compromise	win	work	enjoy	support
help	think	laugh	accomplish	

Cooperating means _____

_____

_____

_____

_____

Now use the back of this paper, and write about a time when you **cooperated with someone to accomplish a goal**, instead of working alone.

Cooperating with Others
Self-Assessment and Group Task

Objectives:

The students will:
— assess their attitudes and behaviors in group situations.
— describe the qualities and abilities they bring to groups.
— list the most important qualities of a group member.

Grades:

4-8

Materials:

one copy of the self-assessment, "The Group and I," for each student; writing materials; several samples of want ads (optional)

Procedure:

Distribute the self-assessments. Explain that you want the students to take a few minutes to evaluate the attitudes and behaviors they have in groups. Answer any questions about procedure and then give the students 5 to 10 minutes to complete the assessment. When the students are finished, assure them that the contents of their self-assessments are private. Ask them to take a few moments to review what they have written, and then fold the sheets over or put them away.

Have the students form groups of four to six. Ask them to think of one thing that they learned from completing the self-assessment that they wouldn't mind sharing with their group. Allow about 15 minutes for sharing.

When they have finished sharing, tell the groups that you want them to work together to write a "want ad" for a qualified group member.

(If you have ad samples, give one to each group.) Tell the groups to list in their ad the most important qualifications a group member should have. Explain that the qualities and abilities they list should be of benefit to almost any kind of group.

When the groups have finished, ask them to share their ads with the rest of the class. Facilitate a class discussion.

Discussion Questions:

1. What are the most important qualities/abilities a person can bring to a group? Why are they so important?
2. How can a group bring out the best in each of its members?
3. Do members of a group always have to agree? Why or why not?
4. What can you do when disagreements and conflict erupt in a group?

The Group and I
Self-Assessment

How do you feel about cooperating with others? What are your actions?

Read each set of statements. Put an **X** on the line to show how you rate yourself.

I tend to avoid group activities.	I take part in group activities as often as possible.

I'm never the first person to start a conversation.	I go out of my way to start conversations with other people.

I prefer to be alone.	I avoid being alone.

When I'm in a group, I don't contribute much.	I contribute a lot to every group I'm with.

I am not an important group member.	My membership in a group is always important.

Think of a time when you helped a group accomplish its goal. List the three most important **qualities** or **abilities** you brought to the group.

1._____

2._____

3._____

Who Can We Count On?

Experience Sheet and Discussion

Objectives:

The students will:
— identify specific ways in which people "count on" one another.
— name specific ways in which they count on individual classmates.
— explain why it is important for people to count on one another.
— define *trust* and explain in simple terms how it develops.

Grades:

1-6

Materials:

one copy of the experience sheet, "Count on Me" (prepared in advance according to the directions, below), for each child; chalkboard and chalk

Preparation:

Make four copies of the experience sheet. Write the first names of one-fourth of your students on each sheet (randomly mixed). Duplicate the prepared copies for distribution (one version per child).

Procedure:

Ask the students to help you brainstorm some of the many different ways people count on one another in the classroom and elsewhere. List their ideas on the chalkboard. To facilitate, ask such questions as, "What do you count on each other for?" "What do you count on me for?" "What do you count on your parents for?" "What do you count on your neighbors for?" "What do you count on law enforcement officers for?" Write their ideas on the chalkboard. Include such items as:

I count on _____ to help me solve problems...
  ...play with me.
  ...make me laugh.
  ...listen when I talk.
  ...keep a secret.
  ...help with chores.
  ...help with schoolwork.
  ...tell the truth.
  ...understand me.
  ...answer my questions.
  ...love me.
  ...pitch in.
  ...be fair in games.
  ...protect me.
  ...do a good job.
  ...be on time.
  ...keep a promise.

Distribute the experience sheet. Explain that you have divided up the names of class members so that everyone's name is on a sheet, but no sheet has all of the names. Tell the students that you want them to think about the unique qualities, talents, and abilities of each person listed on their sheet and write down one way in which they count on that person. Tell them to use the list on the board for ideas and help with spelling. Circulate and provide assistance, as needed.

When the students have finished, ask those whose names are on the first list to come to the front of the room. Stand behind one student at a time and ask: "What do you count on (John) for?" Call on individual students to read what they have written. Repeat this process with the groups of students whose names are on the remaining lists. Conclude with a class discussion.

Discussion Questions:

1. How do you feel knowing that you can count on so many people?
2. How do we learn to count on other people?
3. How do you let others know they can count on you?
4. How does knowing you can count on someone build *trust*? What is trust?

Count on Me!

I can count on _____ to _____ .

I can count on _____ to _____ .

I can count on _____ to _____ .

I can count on _____ to _____ .

I can count on _____ to _____ .

I can count on _____ to _____ .

I can count on _____ to _____ .

I can count on _____ to _____ .

I can count on _____ to _____ .

I can count on _____ to _____ .

My classmates can count on me to:

1. _____

2. _____

3. _____

Experience Sheet

Weighing the Two C's
Discussion and Experience Sheet

Objectives:

The students will:
— distinguish between cooperative and competitive behaviors.
— describe the benefits and drawbacks of cooperative and competitive behaviors.
— identify ways that the class can be more cooperative.

Grades:

4-8

Materials:

one copy of the the experience sheet, "Cooperation and Competition," for each child; chalkboard and chalk

Procedure:

Read the following story to the students.

Mr. Monday's class was getting ready for the science fair. The students worked on their projects every day, independently and quietly. First they researched different project ideas. Then they met individually with Mr. Monday to decide what to work on. If a student couldn't come up with an idea, Mr. Monday assigned one. When the students had a question or got stumped, Mr. Monday often sent them to the library to find answers in reference books. Mr. Monday urged the students to keep their projects under wraps and their findings secret, so that everyone would be surprised on the opening day of the fair. The students assembled their displays at home and didn't bring them to school until the day before the fair. Mr. Monday reminded the students that the judges would be awarding prizes for the best entries.

Ms. Friday's class was getting ready for the science fair, too. First, small groups of students researched possible project topics. Then the groups compiled their ideas in one big list and the entire class chose eight projects to work on. The students formed eight teams. Students who weren't sure which team they wanted to belong to were allowed to work on more than one team until they decided. Ms. Friday encouraged all the teams to share ideas with one another. About once a week, she called an "Investigator's Forum" where each team reported on the status of its project, and where everyone offered suggestions and brainstormed ideas to make the projects better. The groups built their displays in class, sometimes staying after school to put in extra time. There was a lot of moving around in Ms. Friday's class, and quite a bit of noise, too. Ms. Friday told the students that she wanted all the projects to be the best they could be.

Write the headings "Competitive" and "Cooperative" on the chalkboard. Ask the students which label fits Mr. Monday's class and which fits Ms. Friday's class. Then ask them to recall specific attitudes and behaviors in each story that were competitive and cooperative. Write their ideas on the board under the appropriate heading. For example:

Mr. Monday/Competitive

worked alone
kept projects secret
didn't share ideas
concentrated on winning prizes

Ms. Friday/Cooperative

worked in teams
shared ideas
did joint problem-solving
talked freely
concentrated to making all projects excellent

Distribute the experience sheets. Answer any questions about procedure, and give the students a few minutes to complete their sheets. Then, ask the students to form small groups of five to seven and share what they have written. Encourage them to talk about the differences between cooperative and competitive activities, behaviors, and statements. Conclude the activity with a total class discussion.

Discussion Questions:

1. What are the benefits of cooperating with others? What are the drawbacks?
2. What are the benefits of competing with others? What are the drawbacks?
3. What activities are competitive and cooperative at the same time? Which approach is more important in those activities? Why?
4. What specifically can this class do to become more cooperative?

Cooperation and Competition

What do you like to do with friends? Maybe you like to play baseball or chess, talk, tell jokes, go bicycling or skating, dance, hike, bake, build things, or walk around the mall.   On the lines below, write your favorite activities. Then write whether each one is cooperative or competitive.

Activity	Competitive or Cooperative?
1. _____	_____
2. _____	_____
3. _____	_____
4. _____	_____
5. _____	_____

Write one *cooperative* thing you did yesterday or today:

_____

_____

Write one *competitive* thing you did yesterday or today:

_____

_____

What is something you often say that is *cooperative*?

_____

_____

What is something you often say that is *competitive*?

_____

_____

Cooperating on the Job
Interviews and Discussion

Objectives:

The students will:
— identify specific cooperative behaviors of adults in their jobs.
— state why cooperation is important at work.
— describe how cooperative behaviors can be used to resolve conflict.

Grades:

4-8

Materials:

one copy of the interview form for each student; chalkboard and chalk

Procedure:

Write the word *cooperation* on the chalkboard. Review with the students any concepts learned from previous activities involving cooperation/competition.

Ask the students to name some of the ways adults need to cooperate with one another in their jobs. Suggest that they think about working adults they know, like their parents, neighbors, school staff, and employees at stores and theaters they patronize. List their ideas on the chalkboard and discuss.

Distribute the interview forms. Explain that you want each student to interview two adults regarding their work-related cooperative behaviors. One of the adults may be a parent and the other a non-relative, or both may be non-relatives. Answer any questions regarding the interview form. Give the students 2 to 3 days to complete their interviews.

Have the students form groups of four to six and share the results of their interviews. Have them categorize the cooperative behaviors mentioned by the people they interviewed and tally the number of responses in each category. Categories might include cooperating to produce a product, make decisions, sell a product, communicate with customers, etc.

While the small groups take turns reporting their findings to the class, list the major categories of cooperation on the board. Compare this list to the one generated by the class before the interviews, and facilitate a culminating discussion.

Discussion Questions:

1. What would happen if the people we interviewed didn't cooperate with their co-workers?
2. Does cooperating with other people mean that you never have disagreements? Why or why not?
3. How can people handle their disagreements in a cooperative way?
4. Would you prefer to work in a place where people are cooperative most of the time or competitive most of the time? Why?

Cooperating on the Job
Interview Form

Talk with two adults about their jobs. Write down their answers to the following questions.

Name _____ **Job** _____

    1. How many people do you work with in your job? _____

    2. How do you cooperate with these people? _____

        _____

        _____

        _____

        _____

    3. What would happen if you didn't cooperate with your co-workers?

        _____

        _____

Name _____ **Job** _____

    1. How many people do you work with in your job? _____

    2. How do you cooperate with these people? _____

        _____

        _____

        _____

        _____

    3. What would happen if you didn't cooperate with you co-workers?

        _____

        _____

Heart to Heart

Exploring Math Together

Objectives:

The students will:
— practice cooperative group behaviors in completing a math task.
— practice a conflict-management strategy involving communication and negotiation.

Grades:

1-2

Materials:

paper plates (one per group member); a box containing sets of small items such as bottle caps, buttons, paper clips, crayons, keys, and popsicle sticks; fabric; number cards; "Heart Pillow Pattern"; thread and needle (or sewing machine); fiberfill or pillow stuffing

Preparation:

Make a heart pillow using the "Heart Pillow Pattern" (provided). Cut out two heart-shaped pieces of fabric. Place the right sides of the fabric together and sew, leaving a small opening for stuffing. Turn right-side out and stuff with fiberfill. Close the opening with blind stitches.

Procedure:

Gather the students together and explain that they are going to cooperate in groups of four or five to do a math task. Explain that working cooperatively means being kind to one another and, when necessary helping each other. Tell the students that if there are any disagreements or fights, the people involved will have to stop the math activity and have a "heart to heart" talk. Show the students the heart pillow. Explain that during a "heart to heart" talk, the person holding the heart talks, while the other person listens. The person talking tells his or

her side of the story. Then he or she passes the heart to the other person, who tells his or her side of the story. The heart is passed back and forth until feelings are expressed and an agreement is made to cooperate in the group. If the entire group cooperates, then it is not necessary to have any "heart to heart" talks.

Set up groups of four or five. Put a paper plate on the table for each student. Place the box of items on the table, making sure that the quantity of each item equals or exceeds the highest numeral to be explored. Assign each student an item to place on his or her plate. For example, assign one student the buttons, another the keys, another the bottle caps, etc. Show the students a number card. (Choose a number to which the students can easily count.) Tell the students that their task is to find and place that number of items on the plate in front of them. The quantity of the item must match the number on the card. The students can also find and give items to each other. When the

99

students appear to have finished the task, help them check the number of items on each plate by counting them together. Repeat the task using different numbers. Lead a follow-up discussion.

Discussion Questions:

1. What does working cooperatively mean?

2. How did cooperating help you complete the math task?
3. How do "heart to heart" talks help settle conflict?

Extension:

Use the "heart to heart" talk any time conflicts arise and the students need to listen to each other.

Heart Pillow Pattern

Toothpick Towers
A Cooperative Building Experiment

Objectives:

The students will:
— demonstrate cooperative (and competitive) behaviors while completing a task.
— describe how one person's actions affect the actions of others.
— explain how cooperative behaviors aid in goal attainment.

Grades:

K-8

Materials:

approximately 16 toothpicks and one small-necked bottle (8-ounce plastic juice bottles are ideal) for each group

Procedure:

Ask the students to form groups of six to eight and sit in a circle. Give each person two toothpicks. Hand a bottle to one person in each group. Direct that person to place one toothpick across the opening of the bottle and then pass the bottle to the next person. Have that person repeat the procedure using one toothpick. Continue passing the bottle around the circle, adding one toothpick at a time until all of the toothpicks have been successfully placed across the opening of the bottle. Tell the students that if even one toothpick drops, they must start over.

Note on the board how long it takes each group to successfully complete the task. When all of the groups have finished, lead a discussion, focusing on cooperative versus competitive behaviors. If groups have to start over due to competitive behaviors, focus on the resulting frustration and loss of time. (Use time-keeping to document the affects of competitive behavior, not to encourage competition between groups or denote who "wins.")

Discussion Questions:

1. How did you feel when it was your turn to put a toothpick on the bottle?
2. What did you think about when you decided how to place your toothpick?
3. How did your behaviors affect the person who came after you?
4. How did you place your toothpick if you wanted the next person to succeed?
5. How would you have placed your toothpick if you had wanted the next person to fail?
6. How would you pass the bottle if you wanted the next person to succeed? ...to fail?
7. What cooperative behaviors did you see in this activity? What competitive behaviors did you see? Which type of behavior helped your group complete the task?
8. What did you learn from this activity about cooperating with others?

Variations:

For older students, increase the number of toothpicks per student to three. Or have them place straws or pencils across an open box or basket. Very young students could use popsicle sticks.

The Cooperative "Cookbook"
Creative Writing and Discussion

Objectives:

The students will:
— identify and creatively list ingredients of various cooperative relationships.
— explain the importance of knowing the ingredients of something you want to make or be.

Grades:

4-6

Materials:

several samples of recipes, large unlined index cards, writing materials, art materials, large notebook or scrapbook, and glue

Procedure:

Begin by asking how many of your students have ever followed a recipe when baking or cooking something. Explain that a recipe lists necessary ingredients and gives directions for combining and preparing those ingredients. Note that although recipes are traditionally associated with food, they can be written for almost anything. For example, recipes could be developed for a healthy lifestyle, a perfect friendship, a powerful speech, and a winning tennis game.

Announce that the students are going to compile a "Cooperative Cookbook" made up of recipes for different "dishes" in a cooperative world. Generate a list of subjects for possible recipes, such as, cooperative classroom, perfect family, ideal friendship, peaceful world, friendly town, etc. Urge the students to be creative and to keep in mind different types of dishes when they select a title. For example, "Cooperative Classroom Crepes," "Perfect Family Fudge," "Ideal Friendship Salad," "Peaceful World Stew," "Friendly Town Torte," etc.

Allow the students to choose partners if they wish, and distribute the recipe samples. Have the students develop their recipe on scrap paper before printing the final version on the front side of one or more index cards. Circulate and assist.

Ask the students to share their recipes with the class while you facilitate a discussion. Glue the recipes in the notebook or scrapbook and invite volunteers to add illustrations.

Discussion Questions:

1. Why do cooks create and follow recipes?
2. How does it help to develop recipes for things like cooperation and peace?
3. What will happen if we try to create a cooperative classroom without knowing what goes into it?
4. How can we find out the ingredients for something like a cooperative classroom?

How Do Things Stack Up?

A Game of Support

Objectives:

The students will:
— work cooperatively to build a structure out of books.
— draw analogies between the book structures and human support systems.
— explain how cooperation contributes to goal attainment.

Grades:

6-8

Materials:

lots of hardcover books

Procedure:

Divide the class into groups of five or six. Explain that each group will work cooperatively to build a structure out of books. Each book in the structure must support one or more other books. This "house of books" can have many angles and be multi-tiered. Encourage the groups to be imaginative and create their own "architectural masterpieces." Announce the following rules:

- Time will be called at the end of 10 minutes.
- Groups are encouraged to use books of all sizes.
- Members of the group must work cooperatively, contributing an equal number of books to the structure.
- If the structure collapses, the group may start over and continue to work until time is called.

Begin the activity and call time at the end of 10 minutes.

Invite each group to show its structure to the other groups. Let the students talk about what was difficult and what was easy in the construction process. Lead a follow-up discussion, talking about the concepts of mutual support and cooperation. Use the "house of books" as an analogy.

Discussion Questions:

1. What cooperative behaviors did you use in your group?
2. How are the "houses of books" similar to the support systems we have in our lives?
3. What happens when one member of a group "falls" (fails to cooperate with and support others)?
3. How can group members help each other "rebuild" after a conflict or disagreement?
4. How does it feel to have a support system?

Coming to Consensus
Practice in Consensus-Seeking

Objectives:

The students will:
— learn and practice a method for making decisions by consensus.
— state how consensus is different from other decision-making approaches.
— identify the benefits of consensus-seeking.

Grades:

5-8

Materials:

writing materials for the students; chalk-board and chalk

Procedure:

Ask the students to describe all the different ways that members of a group make decisions from among two or more choices. For example:
— voting (majority or two-thirds rule)
— one person makes the decision for everyone else
— no one makes the decision so whatever happens happens

Introduce the students to the concept of *consensus*. Explain that when a group decides by consensus, everyone agrees. Consensus seeking usually takes longer than other methods because the people involved have to discuss the issue and their choices thoroughly before coming up with something everyone can agree on. However, consensus usually gets better results, because all group members buy into the decision and try to make it work.

Have the students form groups of four to six. Tell them that their first task is to choose a recorder, and that they must do it by consensus. Write the following steps on the board and suggest that the students follow them:

1. One person nominates another to be the recorder.
2. After 30 seconds, the members of the group take turns stating whether they agree or disagree with the suggestion.
3. If most people agree, but two firmly disagree, then another name must be suggested.
4. If only one person disagrees, the group talks about the reasons for the disagreement and tries to compromise.

Answer any questions and then signal the groups to begin the process of choosing a recorder. After all the groups have selected a recorder, have them practice several more consensus-seeking rounds, choosing topics from the following list (written on the board).
- five activities that everyone enjoys
- the most difficult thing about school
- three ways that all people are exactly alike
- the two most important ingredients of a winning team
- five good ways to settle an argument
- the ideal Thanksgiving dinner

Direct the recorders to write down the decisions of their group. Allow at least 20 minutes for practice. Then ask the recorders to read their results to the class. Lead a follow-up discussion.

Discussion Questions:

1. What was the hardest thing about reaching consensus? What was easiest?

2. What kinds of problems did your group encounter? How did you resolve them?

3. How did you feel while participating in consensus-seeking? How do those feelings compare to the feelings you get from "majority rules" decisions? ...from other types of decisions?

4. What classroom decisions could be made by consensus? What family decisions?

Connect!

A Cooperative Team Experience

Objectives:

The students will:
— cooperate in solving a problem.
— identify specific cooperative and competitive behaviors and describe how they affect completion of a team task.

Grades:

5-8

Materials:

construction paper or tag board (one color only) with which to make a set of puzzle pieces for each group of players (see "Preparation," below); table and chairs for each group of players

Preparation:

Start with <u>eight</u> 8-inch by 8-inch squares of construction paper or tag board *for each team.* Individually cut each square into three to five smaller pieces (see illustration). Place all of the pieces for one team in a single envelope.

Procedure:

If the entire class is playing, ask the students to form teams of five to eight. Have each team sit around a table, and select one member to be its Observer. Announce that all other team members are players.

Take the Observers aside and say to them: *Your job is to stand beside the table while your team is playing the game and notice what happens. Be prepared to describe such things as how well the group works together, who shares puzzle parts and who does not; whether members concentrate only on the puzzle in front of them or watch the progress of all the puzzles; cooperative vs. competitive behaviors; any conflicts that occur and how they are resolved.*

Read aloud the following rules of play:
• Your task is to assemble eight squares of EQUAL size.
• There will be NO talking, pointing, or other nonverbal communication.
• A player may pass puzzle parts to any other team member at any time.
• You may NOT take, ask for, or indicate in any way that you want another team member's puzzle pieces.
• There is no time limit. the game is over when you have finished the task.

Distribute the puzzle pieces randomly among the players. Give each player approximately the same number of pieces.

Give the signal to start play.

At the conclusion of play, have the Observers give feedback to their team. If several teams are playing, have the Observers do this simultaneously. Advise the teams to listen carefully, and not to interrupt, argue with, or put down the Observer in any way.

Discussion Questions:

1. What did you learn from your Observer?
2. What was the object of the game?
3. Which kind of behavior was most effective in this game, cooperative or competitive? Why?
4. What are some of the effects of competitive behavior on a team? ...of cooperative behavior?
5. If you could play the game again, would you change your own behavior?
6. What did you learn from this experience?

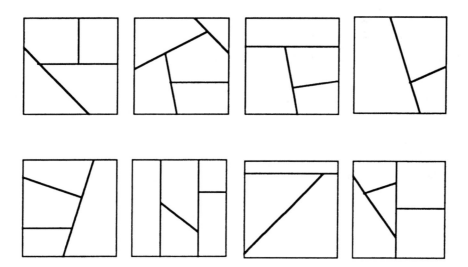

Rules to Live By

An Experiment in Consensus-Seeking

Objectives:

The students will:
— reach consensus on rules of conduct for living in a fictional society.
— describe individual and group behavior during the exercise.
— describe how conflicts were handled during the exercise.

Grades:

5-8

Materials:

writing materials

Procedure:

Divide the class into an even number of small groups, not exceeding six members each. Announce that the groups have been stranded on a desert island with no hope of rescue. Food is plentiful and there is unlimited drinking water. The task is to reach consensus on the following questions about basic government:

A. What will be considered basic human rights?
B. How will decisions be reached?
C. How will cooperation be encouraged?
D. How will conflicts be resolved?

Note: Based on the amount of time you have, limit the number of questions each group considers. (You might want to divide the questions between groups.) Allow 20 minutes of discussion per question.

Have the groups each select one member to write down their decisions.

When the students have reached consensus on their questions, ask each group to share its decisions with one other group. Have the students in the combined groups sit in a circle and select a leader. The leader's job is to conduct the sharing session and make sure that only one person speaks at a time. Allow about 15 minutes for sharing and urge the leaders to divide the time equally between the two groups. Lead a follow-up class discussion.

Discussion Questions:

1. How did your group achieve consensus on its decisions?
2. How were conflicts handled?
3. Did your group's behavior match the rules for behavior it was establishing for the fictional society? What were the differences?
4. Why do groups of people need rules to govern them?

Viewpoints
Presentations and Discussion

Objectives:

The students will:
— present and consider both sides of controversial issues.
— describe how they choose a position on a controversial issue.
— demonstrate respect for opposing positions based on fact.

Grades:

6-8

Materials:

fact cards listing opposing arguments for various issues, props for the presentations (optional)

Preparation:

Identify issues where students have not formed strong opinions, but where different viewpoints exist. For each issue, develop two fact cards, one outlining the supporting position, the other outlining the opposing position. List facts, not opinions. For example, "Prohibiting smoking in restaurants will seriously hurt business" is not a factual statement. However, "Some restaurant owners believe that prohibiting smoking will seriously hurt business" is. Select issues that are appropriate for the age and sophistication of your students. Here are some suggestions:

• Restaurants should/should not be completely nonsmoking.
• Schools should/should not develop dress codes for students.
• The government should/should not assure health care for all citizens.
• Companies should/should not provide fitness centers for employees.
• Students should/should not help establish school rules.
• Motorcycle (bicycle) riders should/ should not be required to wear helmets.

Procedure:

Divide the class into teams of two or three.

Give each team a fact card. Emphasize that the students are to represent the position they have been given, whether or not they agree with it. Have the teams meet and decide how to present their facts. Possibilities include the use of skits, public-service announcements, graphs and charts, etc.

Take one issue at a time and have the opposing teams present their facts. Require that the rest of the class listen attentively without interrupting. After both sides of each issue have been presented, ask for a show of hands from supporters of either side, as well as from people who are undecided. Lead a follow-up discussion.

Discussion Questions:

1. How did your group decide on a way to present its facts?
2. How does it feel to present an argument that you don't personally agree with?
3. Why is it important to listen to both sides of an issue?
4. How do you usually decide which position to take on an issue?
5. Are people who disagree with you, wrong? Why or why not?

We Cooperated to Get It Done

A Sharing Circle

Objectives:

The students will:
— describe a situation in which a goal was met through teamwork.
— describe the importance of cooperation in goal attainment.

Grades:

K-8

Introduce the Topic:

Today we're going to talk about teamwork and what it can accomplish. Our topic is, "We Cooperated to Get It Done."

Think of a time when you worked with a group of people to get something done. You can talk about a team activity in which you've participated here in class, or some other cooperative group experience you've had. Perhaps you belong to a sports team that won a game, or a group of scouts that completed a big project. Maybe your family worked as a team to clean up the house or hold a garage sale. You and some friends may have done something together like cook a meal, plan a party, or hold a bake sale. Tell us what the group was trying to accomplish and how you felt being part of it. Take a few moments to think about it. The topic is, "We Cooperated to Get It Done."

Discussion Questions

1. How did most of us feel about being part of a team?
2. Why is cooperation important when a group of people is working together?
3. What can happen if people don't cooperate?
4. How does working with a team on a school assignment affect the quality of your work?
5. How does it affect your attitude?

A Way I Can Be Counted On

A Sharing Circle

Objectives:

The students will:
— identify attributes that they bring to group situations.
— explain why accountability is important when working with others.

Grades:

K-8

Introduce the Topic:

Our topic for this Sharing Circle is, "A Way I Can Be Counted On." All of us work and play with groups and teams. So all of us know how important it is to be able to count on group and team members. When you are a member of a group or team, how can you always be counted on? Maybe you can be counted to do what you say you will do. Or maybe you can be counted on to attend meetings. Perhaps your teammates can count on you to offer your suggestions and ideas, or to participate in activities. Are you the sort of person who can be counted on to do the job that no one else wants to do? Are you someone a group can count on to liven things up and make others feel good? There are many ways to con-tribute to a group or team. What is yours? Take a few moments to think about it. The topic is, "A Way I Can Be Counted On."

Discussion Questions

1. Why is it so important to be able to count on every member of a group or team?
2. What can happen to a group if members aren't accountable?
3. What role does being accountable play in being successful?
4. How can you become more accountable?
5. How can you help your teammates become more accountable?

Additional Sharing Circle Topics

A Time Someone Accepted and Included Me

A Time I Accepted and Included Someone

Someone I Depend On

A Time I Couldn't Have Done It Alone

Someone I Can Count On

A Skill or Talent I Brought to the Team

A Time I Let Down the Team

My Favorite Team

Something I Did That Helped the Team Succeed

How I Felt When the Other Side Won

We Played a Game and Everybody Won

A Way I Show Respect for Others

How I Show Respect for Myself

We Used Teamwork to Get It Done

Strategies for Resolving Conflict

You'll find little extraordinary about the conflict resolution strategies outlined in this section. They are familiar, common sense ways of dealing with conflict.

You've seen children settle conflicts by sharing and taking turns. You've seen one child make a supposedly threatening face that propelled the other into such fits of laughter that the conflict dissolved in mirth. You've seen kids walk away from conflict because they didn't have the resources to deal with it at the moment, and come back later ready and able to achieve a settlement. And, remarkably, you've seen students work out mutually satisfying solutions through compromise, negotiation, and problem solving.

What's often missing in situations like these is the element of conscious choice. Children (and adults for that matter) often have very limited repertoires for handling conflict. Those who have become adept at using a strategy use the same one over and over—they *always* fight, *always* walk away, *always* make jokes, or *always* seek adult intervention.

The activities in this section offer students the opportunity to become familiar with a range of conflict management strategies, to discuss the relative pros and cons of those strategies, and to practice them safely through role playing and other forms of dramatization. Specifically, these activities are designed to help students:

- recognize different conflict styles.
- identify resolution strategies used in real conflict situations.
- understand the advantages gained by understanding the opposing point of view in a conflict situation.
- experience the role that individual perception plays in conflict.
- practice the use of specific conflict-resolution strategies.
- learn to use problem-solving in conflict situations to achieve creative, win-win results.
- understand how stress contributes to and is a product of conflict.
- identify stress-reduction techniques that can help prevent conflict and reduce its negative effects.

Literature Connections

The books listed below describe internal and external conflicts similar to those that students experience daily, and demonstrate a variety of approaches to conflict resolution. Ask your students to read one or more of the books prior to beginning the activities, or assign them throughout your implementation of this unit and the next two. Read the books aloud to younger students. In both cases, follow up with discussion questions to reinforce learning and stimulate higher-level thinking.

Primary:

Seuss, Dr., *The Sneetches*, illustrated by the author, Random House, 1961.

This humorous, but poignant, story-poem reveals conflicts between its characters that stem from individual differences. The Star-Belly Sneetches snub the Plain-Belly sorts until a salesman comes to town with a star stamping machine, throwing confusion into the community—and ultimate awareness of their folly.

Fox, Mem, *Wilfred Gordon McDonald Partridge*, illustrated by Julie Vivas, Kane/Miller, 1985.

A small boy with four names learns that an elderly neighbor, also with four names, has lost her memory. As he tries to discover the meaning of "memory," Wilfren Gordon gathers his treasures and shares them with "Miss Nancy," helping to restore her memory for a while.

Chapman, Carol, *Herbie's Troubles,* illustrated by Kelly Oechsli, Dutton, 1981.

Six-and-a-half year old Herbie liked his mom, dad, the kids on his block, most vegetables, his baby sister, and school—until he met Jimmy John. Jimmy John did everything in the world to make life miserable for Herbie, who tried to follow the advice of his friends in trying to remedy the situation. Nothing worked until he tried his own solution.

Intermediate:

Spinelli, Jerry, *Fourth Grade Rats*, illustrated by Paul Casale, scholastic, 1991.

Suds Morton, who liked being called a "Third Grade Angel" last year, is faced with a dilemma. Should he now live up to the school-yard chant and act like a "Fourth Grade Rat?" The story is his dilemma and how he solves it.

MacLachlan, Patricia, *Sarah, Plain and Tall*, HarperCollins, 1985.

When father invites a mail-order bride to come and live with them on the prairie, young Caleb and his sister Ana try to help her decide to stay. Sarah helps Pa decide to put his grief over the loss of his wife in the past and allow happiness to reenter his life.

Upper:

Byars, Betsy, *The Eighteenth Emergency*, Viking/Penguin, 1973.

Benjie "Mouse" Fawley is fleeing from the toughest kid in the school after writing Marv's name under a Neanderthal man on a school chart. His best friend, Ezzie, has come up with sure-fire solutions to 17 emergencies, like how to survive attacks of stampeding elephants and hungry crocodiles, but has no solution for this 18th emergency!

Crew, Linda, *Children of the River*, Delacorte Press, 1989.

Seventeen-year-old Sundara fled Cambodia with her aunt's family four years ago to escape the Khmer Rouge army, leaving behind her parents, brother, and sister, and the boy she loved as a child. Now she is torn between the choice to remain faithful to her own people and the choice to adjust to life in her Oregon high school as a "regular" American.

One Conflict with Three Endings

Story and Discussion

Objectives:

The students will:
— distinguish between denial, confrontation, and problem solving as responses to conflict.
— explain why problem solving is preferable to denial and confrontation.

Grades:

K-4

Materials:

writing materials for the variation (see next page)

Procedure:

Read the following story to the students three times—first with Ending 1, then with Ending 2, and finally with Ending 3.

Arturo and David are building a model with LEGOs. Mike comes over and asks if he can join in.

Ending 1:

Arturo says, "Sure." David doesn't like Mike very much and would rather that he didn't join them. Instead of saying anything, he just shrugs his shoulders and keeps working. Whenever Mike makes a suggestion, David says it's "dumb." And two or three times he grabs parts from Mike without asking. After a few minutes of this, Mike asks him what's bugging him. He sighs and says, "Nothing."

Ending 2:

Arturo says, "Sure," but David says, "No way!" Mike asks, "Why not?" David responds, "I hate working with you. You always act like you know everything. You don't listen, and you think your ideas are better than everyone else's."

Mike shouts, "You're a liar. You're just jealous because I'm smarter than you are!" David is mad now and says, "You'd better get out of here before I make you!" Mike says, "On yeah? Try it." David moves around the table toward Mike, who runs to the other side of the room.

Ending 3:

Arturo says, "Sure," but David says, "No way!" Arturo asks, "Why don't you want him to work with us?" David responds, "Because I hate working with him. He always acts like he knows everything. He thinks his ideas are better than everyone else's." Mike points out to Arturo that he and David have been using the LEGOs for a long time, and that they really belong to the class, not just to the two of them. Arturo agrees with Mike and offers to let Mike work with him on the part of the model that he is building. David says, "I guess that's okay, if you promise to listen to my ideas, too." Mike answers, "Sure, I'll listen to you. And I'll work on this side of the model with Arturo. But if I have a suggestion about your part, can I ask you if it's okay to make it?" David grins. "Sure," he says.

Ask the students to describe the differences between the three endings. If necessary, read the endings again and discuss one at a time. Explaining the meaning of new words/concepts, help the students see these differences:

- In the first ending, David is using *denial* to respond to the conflict. He is being *passive*.
- In the second ending, David is using *confrontation* to respond to the conflict. Both he and Mike are being *aggressive*.
- In the third ending, all three boys are using *problem solving* to resolve the conflict. They are being *assertive*.

Discuss the differences between denial (pretending nothing's wrong), confrontation (fighting), and problem solving. Then read additional story starters and ask the class to help you make up three endings to each one—the first using denial, the second using confrontation, and the third using problem solving. Encourage the students to imagine what the characters in the story would say and do using each type of response.

Story starters:

Two children are at home watching television. Each one wants to watch a different program.

Stephanie promised to return an umbrella she borrowed from Carla several weeks ago, but forgets to bring it to school. Carla is upset because the umbrella belongs to her mother who expects it back today.

Manny and Vic share a room. Vic keeps his things picked up, but Manny is careless. Their father says neither one can watch television until the room is clean. Manny figures Vic has to help him clean up his half, but Vic doesn't think it's fair.

It's the first day of school and Lucy wants a desk next to her friend Katrin, but all the desks around Katrin are filled. She asks Richard to move, but Richard likes where he's sitting.

Lead a follow-up discussion.

Discussion Questions:

1. What happens inside us when we bury our feelings—when we *deny* them?
2. What can happen when we lose control of our feelings and lash out at others?
3. What kinds of things would you do and say if you wanted to use problem solving?
4. Who "wins" a conflict when people use denial? ...when they use confrontation? ...when they use problem solving? Why?

Variation: Have older students choose one story starter and write the three endings. Allow them to work in pairs.

Conflicts Happen!
Interviews and Discussion

Objectives:

The students will:
— interview people regarding conflicts they have had.
— identify and evaluate strategies used to resolve conflicts.

Grades:

5-8

Materials:

one copy of the interview form for each student

Procedure:

Announce that the students are going to conduct interviews with adults about conflicts they have had. The person interviewed could be a parent, other relative, neighbor, friend, teacher, religious leader, or coach.

Distribute the interview forms. Explain that side one of the form is for use *during* the interview; side two is for the student to complete *after* the interview. Stress that the students are to listen with particular care to *how* the conflict was resolved. If they don't understand what their interviewee is saying, urge the students to ask questions for clarification. Demonstrate effective ways of seeking additional information (open-ended questions, summarizing, etc.). Set a deadline for completion of the interviews.

Have the students share their findings in groups of four to six. Tell them not to identify the people in the conflict. Suggest that they refer to them as persons A and B, or give them fictitious names. Conclude the activity with a class discussion.

Discussion Questions:

1. What kinds of things seem to lead to conflict?
2. What similarities did you hear in the ways people react to conflict?
3. What methods were most often used to resolve these conflicts?
4. What methods seemed to be most effective?
5. In cases where the conflict was never resolved, how do the people feel now?
6. In cases where the conflict was resolved negatively (for instance, through a fight or one person getting back at the other), how do the people feel now?
7. What have you learned about conflict from this activity?

Conflicts Happen!

Interview Form

Ask an adult to tell you about a conflict he or she had with another person. Write down the adult's answers to these questions, paying special attention to *how* the conflict was resolved:

1. **How did the conflict start?** _____

_____

2. **What was the conflict about?** _____

_____

3. **What was it that you needed or wanted?** _____

_____

4. **What did the other person need or want?** _____

_____

5. **Was the conflict resolved?** _____ **If so, how?** _____

_____

_____

6. **Were you satisfied with the outcome of the conflict?** _____
Why or why not? _____

_____

_____

Conflicts Happen!
Interview Form, Page 2

Which of the following methods were used to resolve the conflict. Put a 4 beside <u>all</u> that apply.

____ Nothing was done, so the conflict was never resolved.

____ One or both people apologized.

____ Both people gave up a little of what they wanted, arriving at a *compromise*.

____ Both people thought of possible solutions, talked them over, and agreed to try the one that sounded best. (*Negotiation* and *Problem Solving*)

____ One person listened while the other person expressed his or her feelings. Just listening made things better.

____ One person said something funny and the other person laughed. The humor made both people feel better and the conflict wasn't so important anymore.

____ One person offered to share or take turns, and the other person accepted.

____ Other _____

_____

_____

Experience Sheet

Another Point of View

Reading, Writing, and Discussion

Objectives:

The students will:
— describe the conflict situation in a familiar folk/fairy tale from the point of view of the villain.
— state that every conflict has at least two points of view.
— describe how understanding all points of view can help resolve conflicts.

Grades:

K-4

Materials:

any copy of the story, *The Three Little Pigs*; a copy of the book, *The True Story of the 3 Little Pigs*, by Jon Scieszca (1989, Viking Kestrel); copies of other traditional folk/fairy tales in which there are villains and victims; pencils and writing paper

Procedure:

Read (or review the plot and characters of) the familiar story, *The Three Little Pigs*. Talk about the point of view from which the story is written. Ask the students to identify the villain and victims in the story. Explain: *We are inclined to sympathize with the pigs and think of the wolf as the bad character in the story. However, if we look at the situation from a different point of view, we may change our minds.*

Read aloud the book, *The True Story of the 3 Little Pigs*, told from the wolf's point of view. Make a story map on the board showing the characters, setting, and sequence of events in the story. Talk about how the wolf was innocently trying to borrow a cup of sugar when he accidently sneezed in each situation, creating a series of disasters. Ask the students if, having heard the wolf's account of what happened, they view the story differently.

Tell the students that they are going to have an opportunity to rewrite a well-known folk story or fairy tale from the villain's point of view. Suggest that they reread or think about a story which has both a villain and a victim. Some suggestions might be *Cinderella, Hansel and Gretel, Little Red Riding Hood, Rapunzel,* and *Snow White.* Ask the students to rethink the story from the villain's point of view, and then rewrite it. For example, they might want to rewrite *Cinderella* from a stepsister's point of view, or *Hanzel and Gretel* from the witch's viewpoint. Remind the students to be as convincing as possible, making the reader sympathize with the "alleged" villain. Give them plenty of time to read, think, discuss, and/ or brainstorm with a partner before writing.

On the following day or in the next session, ask the students to read their stories aloud to a partner. Then ask several volunteers to read their stories to the entire class. After each story, talk about the convincing opinions and remarks that cause the class to feel sympathy for the villain.

Lead a discussion about the benefits of seeing a conflict or problem from the other person's point of view.

Discussion Questions:

1. Why is it important to try to see a conflict from all points of view?
2. How can thinking about the other person's point of view help you avoid an argument or conflict?
3. In what kinds of conflict situations should you *not* attempt to understand the other person's point of view?

Variation:

Help kindergarten students develop the alternative story orally, while you write it in large letters on chart paper, perhaps composing a Big Book. Have first graders write their stories in cooperative-learning groups.

Extension:

Ask the students to think of a time when they had a conflict or problem with another person. Have them imagine what the other person was thinking and feeling in the situation. Invite volunteers to share their conflict situation with the class, describing it from both points of view.

Seeing the Same Thing Differently

Discussion and Experience Sheet

Objectives:

The students will:
— describe how different points of view contribute to conflict.
— discuss how recognizing and appreciating different points of view can prevent and resolve conflict.

Grades:

5-8

Materials:

pens or pencils; chalkboard or chart paper; a stop watch or watch with a second hand; one copy of the experience sheet, "Now You Don't See It . . .Now You Do!"

Procedure:

Explain to the students that they are going to experience how easily conflicts can arise from the need of people to be right. In your own words, explain: *Two or more people can be looking at exactly the same thing (e.g., a problem, a question, a statement, etc.) and see it quite differently. This is one of the ways in which people are unique. As we grow older, the way we see things in our world is determined more and more by our previous experiences and learnings. The way we say a particular word can be different, just because of the way we learned it. People even tie their shoes and use their knife and fork in many different ways.*

Offer this observation about conflict: Conflict occurs when people start to argue about the different ways they see things.

Distribute the experience sheets. Ask the students to carefully read the statement, "FINISHED FILES ARE THE RESULT OF YEARS OF SCIENTIFIC STUDY COMBINED WITH THE EXPERIENCE OF MANY YEARS." After they have read the statement, ask the students to count the number of **F**'s it contains. Allow exactly 15 seconds for the students to count—then tell them to turn their experience sheet over so that it is face down.

Take a poll. Ask the students to raise their hands if they saw three **F**'s. Record the number on the board. Then ask for a show of hands from those who saw four **F**'s. Record that number. Finally, ask for a show of hands from those who saw five or more **F**'s. Record that number.

Point out to the students that even though they were looking at exactly the same statement, they saw it differently from one another. Ask the students to again read the statement and count the **F**'s. Allow 5 seconds—then tell them to turn their experience sheet face down again.

Repeat the poll and record the new numbers. Again, point out that even after this second counting, there are differences in perception. Finally, have the students look at the statement together. Read it with them and point out each of the six **F**'s as they appear.

Ask the students to complete the experience sheet. Then generate a follow-up discussion, emphasizing that the need to be right is one of the biggest causes of conflict.

Discussion Questions:

1. What kinds of things do you see differently from other people you know?

2. What happens when people argue about their different views?

3. Have you ever thought you were right about something and then learned later that you were wrong? How did it happen? How did you feel about changing your mind?

4. What do you think is the biggest reason people fight about things?

Now You Don't See It . . . Now You Do!

Read this . . .

FINISHED FILES ARE THE RESULT OF YEARS OF SCIENTIFIC STUDY COMBINED WITH THE EXPERIENCE OF MANY YEARS.

People are different from one another in many ways. How they see things, or what we call their *perceptions*, can be very different even when they are looking at the same thing. This is one important way people are unique.

People sometimes disagree, or argue, about the different ways they see things. Write about an argument you had because you and someone else had different views:

_____

_____

_____

_____

_____

_____

_____

That Settles It!

Role Playing Conflict Strategies

Objectives:

The students will:
— describe and discuss causes of conflict.
— demonstrate ways of coping with conflicts.

Grades:

K-4

Materials:

chalkboard and chalk; copies of the experience sheets, "Sharing and Taking Turns," "Expressing Apologies," and "Listening and Compromising" for each studen (grades 1 and up)

Procedure:

Write the word *conflict* on the chalkboard. Tell the students that a conflict is a disagreement between two or more people. Give some examples, and point out that sometimes conflicts lead to fights. Talk to the students about how situations that might cause a fight can be resolved. Suggest the following ideas:

• People can share or take turns.
• One person can stop arguing and listen carefully to the other.
• One person can say that he or she is sorry.
• They can flip a coin or draw straws.
• They can ask someone to help them.
• Both people can decide to compromise—have (or do) a little of what each person wants.

Tell the students that you are going to read some conflict stories. Urge them to listen carefully; then read the following stories, one at a time. After each story, ask the students which conflict resolution strategy they would use to resolve the problem. Briefly discuss each suggestion, asking

the students to imagine what might happen if it were used. When most of the students (and you) agree that a particular strategy might work, ask some volunteers to act out the story, using the selected strategy.

Conflict Stories:

Two children are building a robot with LEGO parts. One wants the robot to have three arms and two legs. The other wants it to have one arm and move on wheels. They start to argue.

At recess, three students are bouncing the ball to each other, but one is throwing it too hard, making the other two miss. The other two are getting angry. What can they do to resolve the situation?

Three children are at home watching television. Each one wants to watch a different program and they are arguing over who will get his or her way. How can they solve the conflict?

125

Two students are sitting at their desks at school. One forgot to do her homework. She wants to get it done before school starts and the teacher checks for it. The second student wants to talk about an upcoming birthday party and who will be invited. The first student snaps at the second to be quiet and the second doesn't understand what she did wrong. What can both students do?

A child comes to school the day after his pet dog has died. He is upset, but won't tell anyone because he is afraid he might cry. His friend asks to borrow his colored markers and he shouts, "No, you always lose them!" The friend knows that he has never lost a marker and starts to shout back. What can they do?

Invite volunteers to act out at least one resolution to each situation. After each role play, lead a class discussion.

Discussion Questions:

1. Why do you think that this solution would or would not solve the problem?
2. In what other ways could a person handle this situation?
3. How do you think the people in this conflict would feel about this decision?
4. Why is it helpful to talk about and act out these situations, even if they haven't happened yet?

Follow-up:

For readers: Distribute one set of experience sheets and give the students a few minutes to complete them. Circulate and assist, as necessary. Distribute the other two sets of experience sheets on subsequent days.

Sharing and Taking Turns

Sharing and taking turns can help prevent and solve conflicts.

How willing are you to share?

I share equipment and books at school.

_____ Sometimes _____ Always _____ Never

I share the T.V. at home.

_____ Sometimes _____ Always _____ Never

I ask other kids to join in my games.

_____ Sometimes _____ Always _____ Never

I don't mind if my best friend plays with someone else.

_____ Sometimes _____ Always _____ Never

I offer to share my lunch and snacks.

_____ Sometimes _____ Always _____ Never

How willing are you to take turns?

I listen so other people can talk.

_____ Sometimes _____ Always _____ Never

I pass the ball during games.

_____ Sometimes _____ Always _____ Never

I raise my hand before I speak in class.

_____ Sometimes _____ Always _____ Never

I wait in line until it's my turn.

_____ Sometimes _____ Always _____ Never

I don't swing too long if someone else is waiting.

_____ Sometimes _____ Always _____ Never

Experience Sheet

Expressing Apologies

Apologizing can help prevent and solve conflicts.

How do you usually apologize to someone?

____ I talk to the person and say, "I'm sorry."

____ I send a card, letter, or gift to the person.

____ I smile and act friendly toward the person.

____ I give the person a hug.

____ Other. _____

How do you like someone to apologize to you?

____ Talk to me and say he or she is sorry.

____ Send a card, letter, or gift to me.

____ Smile and be friendly to me.

____ Give me a hug.

____ Other. _____

Do you express apologies the same way you like to receive apologies?

____ Yes   ___ No   ___ Sometimes

Listening and Compromising

Listening to someone can help prevent and solve conflicts.

How well do you listen?

I look at the person who is talking.

_____ Sometimes _____ Always _____ Never

I pay attention and try not to think about other things.

_____ Sometimes _____ Always _____ Never

I don't interrupt.

_____ Sometimes _____ Always _____ Never

I try to understand what the person is saying and feeling.

_____ Sometimes _____ Always _____ Never

I try to show the person that I understand.

_____ Sometimes _____ Always _____ Never

Offering to compromise can help solve conflicts.

How willing are you to compromise?

I don't try to have everything my way.

_____ Sometimes _____ Always _____ Never

I ask other people what they want.

_____ Sometimes _____ Always _____ Never

I listen to their ideas.

_____ Sometimes _____ Always _____ Never

I try to find things we can agree on.

_____ Sometimes _____ Always _____ Never

Experience Sheet

Exploring Alternatives to Conflict
Dramatizations and Discussion

Objectives:

The student will learn and practice specific strategies for resolving conflict.

Grades:

5-8

Materials:

a copy of one scenario (from the list on the next page) for each group of students; one copy of the experience sheet, "Conflict Resolution Strategies," for each student

Procedure:

On the board, write the heading "Strategies for Resolving Conflict." Explain to the students that in conflict situations, certain kinds of behaviors tend to help people solve their problems. List the strategies shown below, and make sure that the students understand them. Give examples, and ask the students to describe problems that might be resolved by each alternative.

- **Sharing:** Using/doing something with another person.
- **Taking turns:** Alternately using/doing something with another person.
- **Active Listening:** Hearing the other person's feelings or opinions.
- **Postponing:** Deciding to put off dealing with the conflict until another time.
- **Using humor:** Looking at the situation in a comical way; making light of the situation.
- **Compromising:** Giving up part, in order to get the remainder, of what one wants.
- **Expressing regret:** Saying that you are sorry about the situation, without taking the blame.

- **Problem solving:** Discussing the problem; trying to find a mutually acceptable solution.

Divide the class into small groups and give each group a written conflict scenario. Instruct the groups to discuss the scenario and pick a conflict management strategy from the list of alternatives on the board. Have the members of each group act out the conflict and its resolution, while the rest of the class tries to guess which alternative they are using.

At the conclusion of the role plays, lead a class discussion.

Discussion Questions:

1. Why is it better to practice positive alternatives, rather than wait for a conflict to occur and *then* try them?
2. Which strategies are hardest to use and why? Which are easiest? Which work best and why?
3. At what point do you think you should get help to resolve a conflict?

Conflict Scenarios

Your group is working on a social studies project. You are drawing and coloring a map of the original 13 colonies. As a final step, you plan to print the names and founding dates of the colonies, along with the title of the map. However, another group member also wants to do the printing. The two of you start arguing about who should get the job and other group members take sides. The situation becomes very tense and noisy and the project is in danger of being ruined. Your teacher approaches the group and warns you to solve the problem—or forget the project.

You plan to go to the movies on Saturday afternoon with a friend. Your family suddenly decides to hold a yard clean-up on Saturday, and this makes you very upset. You start to argue with your parents, insisting that since you have done your chores all week, you deserve to spend your allowance on a Saturday afternoon movie. Besides, your friend's parent has offered to drive you to and from the movie theater. You are in danger of being put on restriction because you are starting to yell at your parents.

Without realizing it, you dropped (and lost) your homework on the way to school. That has put you in a bad mood. At recess, a classmate accidently hits you in the back with a soccer ball. You react in anger and threaten to beat up your classmate after school. This makes the classmate angry and he or she reluctantly agrees to fight. Other classmates cheer. They are ready to stay after school to watch the fight. During lunch, you have a chance to think about it. Your realize that you picked the fight because you were upset about your lost homework. You didn't like being hit by the ball, but think that maybe it isn't worth a fight.

You make plans with a few friends to meet a half hour before school to play a quick game of soccer in the school yard. You get up early, but decide to play Nintendo instead of meeting your friends. When you get to school, your friends are angry. They say you messed up the game by making one of the teams a person short. They want you to know that you let them down. Before they can express their feelings, you start making excuses. You don't give them a chance to talk. They start to walk away.

Two students share a locker at school. One of the students is in a rush one day and unknowingly leaves the locker open. When the second student discovers the open locker an hour later, a jacket, a pair of sneakers, and a cassette tape are missing. The second student blames the first, who denies responsibility. They start to fight.

Conflict Resolution Strategies

Have you ever been in a conflict? Of course! No matter how much you try to avoid them, conflicts happen. They are part of life. What makes conflicts upsetting and scary is not knowing how to handle them. If you don't know something helpful to do, you may end up making things worse. So study these strategies, and the next time you see a conflict coming, try one!

1. Share. Whatever the conflict is over, keep (or use) some of it yourself, and let the other person have or use some.

2. Take turns. Use or do something for a little while. Then let the other person take a turn.

3. Active Listen. Let the other person talk while you listen carefully. Really try to understand the person's feelings and ideas. (This boy is talking in American Sign Language.)

4. Postpone. If you or the other person are very angry or tired, put off dealing with the conflict until another time.

5. Use humor. Look at the situation in a comical way. Don't take it too seriously.

6. Compromise. Offer to give up part of what you want and ask the other person to do the same.

7. Express regret. Say that you are sorry about the situation, *without* taking the blame.

8. Problem solve. Discuss the problem and try to find a solution that is acceptable to both you and the other person.

Experience Sheet

Conflicts Can Be Solved!

Practice in Problem Solving

Objectives:

The students will discuss and practice a problem-solving process to use in resolving conflicts.

Grades:

4-8

Materials:

one copy of the experience sheet, "How to Problem-Solve a Conflict," for each student; chalkboard and chalk

Procedure:

Distribute the experience sheets. Read and discuss each step of the problem-solving process with the class.

Steps in Problem-Solving

1. **Stop all blaming.** Blaming each other will not solve the problem. It's a waste of time. Put your energy into working out a solution.

2. **Define the problem.** Ask each other this question: "How do you see the problem?" Then *listen* to each other's answer.

3. **Consider asking for help.** Sometimes it helps to ask a third person to work with you to solve the problem. Choose someone who will listen to both of you and not take sides.

4. **Think of alternative solutions.** Think of as many ideas for solving the problem as you can. It may help to write them down.

5. **Evaluate the alternatives.** Ask yourselves, "What will happen if we try this one?" Be very honest with yourselves and each other.

6. **Make a decision.** Choose the alternative that looks like it has the best chance of working. Don't hesitate to combine parts of two or more alternatives.

7. **Follow through.** Stick with your decision for a reasonable length of time. If it doesn't work, get together and choose a different solution. If the decision causes more problems, solve those, too.

Ask the students to form groups of four. Instruct them to think of a conflict situation between two people that might be resolved using problem solving. (Conflicts from their own experience are okay, as long as the other parties involved remain anonymous.) Tell the students that two members of the group are to go through the problem-solving steps while the other two coach them. If time permits, have the students switch roles and practice the steps again, using a different problem. Conclude the activity with a class discussion.

Discussion Questions:

1. What happens when you get bogged down in the blaming game?
2. Why is it so important to know exactly what the problem is?
3. When should you ask a third person to help you?
4. What is the advantage of thinking of alternative solutions?
5. Why not just do the first thing that comes to mind?
6. Why is it important to imagine what will happen as a result of trying each alternative?
7. If you can't make a decision, which steps could you return to? (2., 4., 5., and 3., in that order. The problem may be incorrectly defined; you may need to think of more alternatives; the consequences may need more thought; or help may be called for.)

How to Problem-Solve a Conflict

Steps in the Problem-Solving Process

1. Stop all blaming. Blaming each other will not solve the problem. It's a waste of time. Put your energy into working out a solution.

2. Define the problem. Ask each other this question: "How do you see the problem?" Then *listen* to each other's answer.

3. Consider asking for help. Sometimes it helps to ask a third person to work with you to solve the problem. Choose someone who will listen to both of you and not take sides.

4. Think of alternative solutions. Think of as many ideas for solving the problem as you can. It may help to write them down.

5. Evaluate the alternatives. Ask yourselves, "What will happen if we try this one?" Be very honest with yourselves and each other.

6. Make a decision. Choose the alternative that looks like it has the best chance of working. Don't hesitate to combine parts of two or more alternatives.

7. Follow through. Stick with your decision for a reasonable length of time. If it doesn't work, get together and choose a different solution. If the decision causes more problems, solve those, too.

Stress and Conflict

Self-Assessment and Discussion

Objectives:

The students will:
— define stress and identify sources of stress in their own life.
— explain how stress can lead to conflict.
— describe positive techniques for handling stress.

Grades:

4-8

Materials:

one copy of the self-assessment, "Stress and Me," for each student

---

Procedure:

Begin by discussing the relationship between stress and conflict:

When a person is under too much stress—feeling tired, worried, or pressured—he or she is more likely to get into conflicts than when feeling rested, confident, and in control. By the same token, conflicts, when they occur, are usually quite stressful. Consequently, knowing ways to reduce stress may, 1) prevent conflicts and, 2) make them less upsetting when they occur.

Distribute the self-assessments. Go over the directions and give the students 5 to 10 minutes to write down their responses.

Engage the students in a discussion about methods of handling stress. Point out that when the students are experiencing stress, they need to identify what is bothering them so they can eliminate the problem and/or effectively cope with the stress. They need to define the problem, confront it, and take action. Empha-

size, however, that not all stressors can be eliminated. Some can't even be reduced. If their parents are getting a divorce, for example, the students have little or no control over the situation. Therefore, they must concentrate on reducing their stress *reaction*.

Ask the students to help you brainstorm effective methods of reducing stress. List their ideas on the board. Include such items as:

- Sleep.
- Read a book.
- Ask for a hug.
- Go to a movie.
- Listen to music.
- Play with a pet.
- Go for a jog or walk.
- Eat nutritious foods.
- Scream into a pillow.
- Clean out your closet.
- Volunteer to help others.
- Talk with a friend or helpful adult.
- Breath deeply, meditate, or do yoga.
- Stretch, do aerobic exercise, or dance.

If time permits, have the students form groups of three and discuss their self-assessments. Suggest that they compare items to discover similarities and differences, and then select one item on which they all circled the number **5**. Ask them to discuss what they are doing, or could do, to decrease stress in that area. Conclude with a class discussion.

Discussion Questions:

1. What is stress?
2. What causes stress?
3. Why is it important to learn ways of reducing stress?
4. How does stress contribute to conflict?
5. How does stress reduction help prevent conflict?

Stress and Me

Read this list of possible stressors and decide, on a scale of 1 to 5, how concerned you are about each one. Circle 1 on the scale if you never experience this kind of stress. Circle 5 on the scale if you experience this kind of stress frequently and in large doses.

1 2 3 4 5   **1. I am concerned about my grades.**

1 2 3 4 5   **2. I am concerned about my appearance.**

1 2 3 4 5   **3. I am concerned about being lonely.**

1 2 3 4 5   **4. I am concerned about not fitting in at school.**

1 2 3 4 5   **5. I am concerned about making friends.**

1 2 3 4 5   **6. I am concerned about losing a friend.**

1 2 3 4 5   **7. I am concerned about being shy.**

1 2 3 4 5   **8. I am concerned about my health.**

1 2 3 4 5   **9. I am concerned about the health of a family member.**

1 2 3 4 5   **10. I am concerned about money.**

1 2 3 4 5   **11. I am concerned about my parents divorcing.**

1 2 3 4 5   **12. I am concerned about my weight.**

1 2 3 4 5   **13. I am concerned about disappointing my parents.**

1 2 3 4 5   **14. I am concerned about dying.**

1 2 3 4 5   **15. I am concerned about a specific subject or teacher.**

1 2 3 4 5   **16. I am concerned about alcohol or drugs.**

1 2 3 4 5   **17. I am concerned about a specific friend.**

1 2 3 4 5   **18. I am concerned about my safety.**

1 2 3 4 5   **19. I am concerned about responsibilities I have.**

1 2 3 4 5   **20. I am concern about . . .**

Experience Sheet

Conflicts I've Managed

Dyads and Discussion

Objectives:

The students will:
— describe conflict resolution strategies they have used.
— discuss the effectiveness of conflict resolution strategies in different situations.

Grades:

5-8

Materials:

chart paper and magic markers or chalkboard and chalk

Procedure:

Ask the students to choose partners and sit facing each other. Tell the partners to get as far away from other pairs as possible, to reduce distractions. Explain that you are going to give them several topics that involve the use of conflict management strategies. Both partners will speak for 2 minutes on each topic. Tell the students that you will call time every 2 minutes. Urge them not to interrupt each other or ask unnecessary questions. Suggest they alternate being the first speaker.

Announce the topics one at a time, writing them on chart paper or the chalkboard. Briefly discuss the intent of each topic and give examples, as needed. (See suggestions in parentheses, below.)

Topics

"I Shared Something I Wanted for Myself"
(Children are admonished to share starting at a very young age. Remind the students of this fact.)

"A Time Somebody Was Mad at Me,
But Calmed Down
After I Listened to Him/Her"
(This topic relates to the effectiveness of active listening in diffusing strong feelings, whereas arguing, criticizing, and blaming generally aggravate them.)

"A Time I Apologized,
But I Didn't Take the Blame"
(This topic is intended to illustrate that a person can express regret and sympathy, while still making it clear that she or he did not cause the problem.)

"It looked As If a Fight Might Start,
So We Put It Off"
(This topic is based on the notion that when one or both persons in a conflict are tired or overcome by negative feelings, a wise strategy is often to postpone any discussion until a later time.)

"Instead of Fighting,
We Ended Up Laughing"
(This topic addresses the effectiveness of humor, jokes, and clowning in conflict situations.)

"A Time I Managed a Conflict by Negotiating or Compromising"
(This topic suggests that both parties may be able to win in a conflict situation if they are willing to participate in problem solving, or are willing to *give up* part of what they want in order to *get* part of what they want.

Reconvene the class. Facilitate a class discussion.

Discussion Questions:

1. Which conflict resolution strategy have you used most often? ...least often? Why?
2. What happens when you try to ignore a conflict?
3. What can you do if the other person refuses to try to resolve the conflict?
3. What was the most meaningful part of this activity for you?

I Observed a Conflict

A Sharing Circle

Objectives:

The students will:
— describe a conflict situation they observed.
— discuss the dynamics of conflict.
— describe feelings generated in conflict situations.

Grades:

K-8

Introduce the Topic:

Today we're going to talk about conflict situations we've witnessed. Our topic is, "I Observed a Conflict."

There probably isn't anyone here who hasn't at some point in his or her life watched some kind of conflict taking place. A conflict can have many forms. It can be an argument between two people over who has the best idea for a project, or who needs the car more. It can be a squabble over who gets the last cookie. Some conflicts are fights or arguments that involve some kind of violence or the threat of it. Still other conflicts take place inside one person; for example, when someone is torn between two choices, like who to vote for, what to do on the weekend, or who to live

with after a divorce. Think of a conflict that you observed. It could have been between friends, family members, or strangers. Without actually telling us who was involved, or your relationship to the people, tell us what happened. The topic is, "I Observed a Conflict."

Discussion Questions:

1. Why do we have conflicts?
2. What kinds of things happened in most of the conflicts we shared?
3. Why is it sometimes difficult to think clearly when you get involved in an argument?
4. Is it possible for both people to win in a conflict? How?

I Got Into a Conflict

A Sharing Circle

Objectives:

The students will:
— describe conflicts they have experienced and what caused them.
— describe ways of dealing with the feelings of others in conflict situations.
— identify strategies for resolving conflicts with peers and adults.

Grades:

K-8

Introduce the Topic:

Our topic today is, "I Got Into a Conflict." Conflicts are very common. They occur because of big and little things that happen in our lives. And sometimes the littlest things that happen can lead to the biggest conflicts. This is your opportunity to talk about a time when you had an argument or fight with someone. Maybe you and a friend argued over something that one of you said that the other didn't like. Or maybe you argued with a brother or sister over what T.V. show to watch, or who should do a particular chore around the house. Have you ever had a fight because someone broke a promise or couldn't keep as secret? If you feel comfortable telling us what happened, we'd like to hear it. Describe what the other person did and said, and what you did and said. Tell us how you felt and how the other person seemed to feel. There's just one thing you shouldn't tell us and that's the name of the other person, okay? Take a few moments to think about it. The topic is, "I Got Into a Conflict."

Discussion Questions:

1. How did most of us feel when we were part of a conflict?
2. What kinds of things led to the conflicts that we shared?
3. How could some of our conflicts have been prevented?
4. What conflict management strategies could have been used in the situations that we shared?

Additional Sharing Circle Topics

I Observed a Conflict

I Almost Got into a Fight

I Got Blamed for Something I Didn't Do

I Got Involved in a Conflict Because Something Unfair
Was Happening to Someone Else

A Time I Controlled Myself and the Situation Well

A Time I Was Involved in a Misunderstanding

A Time Someone Put Me Down, But I Handled It Well

I Accidentally Made Somebody Mad

I Started a Conflict Between My Friends

Using the Tools of Conflict Resolution

By the time you reach this section of the book, your students will be familiar with a variety of strategies for resolving conflict. This is the time to begin transferring to them responsibility for choosing which strategy to use.

One popular approach involves combining a modified Sharing Circle process with role play, giving students opportunities to 1) describe real conflicts, and 2) act out positive strategies suggested by their classmates. You will find the safe setting of established Sharing Circle groups ideal for this process, particularly when working with younger children.

Peer mediation is a tool which has gained wide acclaim in recent years, and deservedly so. When the adult-child (or authority) element is removed from intervention, everyone ends up on the same psychological plane and all parties tend to approach conflict resolution more responsibly. And, as is almost always the case in helping relationships, the mediators gain as much from the process as do the disputants.

If you already have a peer mediation program in place, consider using the four activities provided as part of your training. If you are considering such a program, you will no doubt devote considerable time and energy to planning,

as well as to the selection and training of peer mediators. A number of excellent resources are available to help you do this, and the activities provided here can be integrated into your program. If you neither have nor plan to start a peer mediation program, by all means use the four peer-mediation activities anyway. They offer numerous benefits to students learning to resolve their own conflicts, as well as those of others.

Activities in this section are designed to help students:

- share real conflicts and act out suggestions for resolving them.
- use puppets as surrogates in dramatizing actual conflict situations.
- observe real conflicts and identify the strategies used.
- resolve conflicts posed anonymously by classmates.
- learn a process for peer mediation.
- practice identifying the problem in conflict situations.
- recognize that conflicts often have several parts and learn to seek resolutions that address all parts.
- learn to distinguish between the needs of disputants and their solutions or positions.

Kids and Conflicts

Sharing Circle with Role Play

Objectives:

The students will:
— describe a real conflict.
— describe alternative suggestions for resolving the conflicts of others.
— demonstrate conflict resolution strategies through role playing.

Grades:

K-8

Materials:

paper and pencil for jotting down the suggestions of students

Procedure:

Note: By combining a modified Sharing Circle process with role play, this activity allows students to explore alternative solutions to real conflicts. Because of the dramatizations involved, you will probably want to keep the groups relatively small.

Have four or five students form a Sharing Circle group. Review the ground rules, and then introduce the topic, as follows:

Our topic for today is, "A Conflict I'm Trying to Resolve." This circle session is a little different from most. Today we're going to have an opportunity to share a conflict or problem that we are having right now and would like some suggestions for solving. After everyone has shared, we'll go back and take a closer look at each conflict. If it's Mary's conflict, for example, we'll start by reviewing what she said to make sure that we understand the situation. Then each of us will take a turn offering Mary one suggestion for
resolving her conflict. Mary will pick the suggestion that she likes best, and role play that suggestion with the help of the group.

Think of a conflict or problem that you are having right now. Maybe you and a friend can't agree on what to do after school, or perhaps you have been fighting a lot with your brother or sister at home. Maybe you had an argument on the playground (in gym) today, or you've had a disagreement with another student about a Math problem or English assignment. The conflict could even be inside yourself. For example, you may be finding it difficult to make a decision about something. Take a few moments to think of a conflict that you don't mind sharing and would like some suggestions for solving. The topic is, "A Conflict I'm Trying to Resolve."

After all of the students who wish to have shared, go back to the first person. Ask a volunteer to review to that person, briefly describing the situation and the conflict. Then ask the students to each offer one suggestion for resolving the conflict. Stress to the students that the resolution needs to be positive. (Initially, plan to be a member of each circle so that you can help the students understand which alternatives are positive and that negative alternatives are not acceptable.) Ask the person whose conflict it is to choose one alternative to role play. Assign parts and carry out the role play immediately, coaching as needed. Then proceed one at a time to all of the remaining conflicts, following the same steps. If time allows, do another round of role plays, dramatizing a second alternative for each conflict. Lead a summary discussion.

Discussion Questions:

1. How well do you think our solutions will work? Why?
2. Why is it important to think of different alternatives for resolving a conflict?
3. What have you learned about resolving conflict from this activity?

NOTE: Combining a Sharing Circle with a role play depicting positive alternatives is a very powerful process for teaching children pro-social conflict resolution strategies. We recommend you use this process a number of times with your students. Choose topics from the following list or create your own.

Additional Sharing Circle topics:

"A Time I Was Involved in a Conflict"
"I Observed a Conflict"
"A Time I Was Involved in a Misunderstanding"
"A Time I Almost Got Into a Fight"
"I Got Involved in a Conflict Because Something Unfair Was Happening to Someone Else"
"A Time I Was Angry at One Person But Took It Out On Someone Else"
"I Got Blamed for Something I Didn't Do"
"I Thought I Was Doing the Right Thing, But I Got Into a Conflict Anyway"

Conflict Theater
Puppet Role Plays

Objectives:

The students will:
- — define the conflict issue in dramatized versions of classroom conflicts.
- — describe and demonstrate alternatives for resolving the conflict.
- — identify effective alternatives and state why they work.

Grades:

K-3

Materials:

several puppets of any type

Procedure:

Keep several puppets on hand to use when conflict erupts between students in the classroom. Let the class name the puppets if they wish. The more you use the puppets, the more the students will come to accept them as conflict-resolution "aides."

When a conflict occurs in the classroom and the students involved do not resolve it within a reasonable length of time, gather the class together and take out one puppet to represent each person in the conflict.

Reenact the conflict, using the puppets. Depending on the age and maturity of your students, you may accomplish this in any of four ways:
1. Have the students in the conflict use the puppets to role play themselves.
2. Have the students in the conflict switch roles and use the puppets to role play each other.
3. Have other volunteers use the puppets to enact the two roles.
4. Enact the roles yourself.

Freeze the puppet play at various points, and ask the audience to summarize what is happening. For example, freeze the action when it becomes clear what each party in the conflict wants or needs; freeze it again when the conflict reaches its height. Ask the class to offer suggestions as to what the puppets could do to resolve their conflict. Incorporate one of these suggestions and complete the role play. Try other suggestions and see how they work. Conclude the puppet play and facilitate a follow-up class discussion.

Discussion Questions:

1. Which suggestion worked best, and why?
2. Which suggestions didn't work, and why?
3. What should you do when you are in a conflict with someone?
4. Is it okay to have conflicts? Why or why not?

Conflict du Jour

Observations and Discussion

Objectives:

The students will:
— describe five conflicts that they have observed.
— identify and evaluate the conflict-resolution strategies and methods used.

Grades:

4-8

Materials:

one copy of the "Conflict Observation Sheet" for each student; chalkboard and chalk

Procedure:

Distribute the "Conflict Observation Forms" Go over the instructions.

Explain that the students are to observe five conflicts, one each day for a week. The observed conflicts may occur between students at school, family members at home, characters on a T.V. show, etc.

Stress that the students are not to get involved; they are to observe silently. After each conflict, the students should immediately record their observations and answer the questions on the form.

The following week, ask the students to take out their completed observation forms. Have them form groups of four to six and share their observations. Ask the groups to tally the number of times each method or strategy was used to end a conflict. Have the groups report their findings, while you record numbers and observations on the board. Facilitate discussion.

Discussion Questions:

1. How did you feel when you were observing other people's conflicts?
2. What kinds of things did people most often do that were helpful?
3. What kinds of things did people do that were hurtful?
4. What kinds of things were least effective?
5. How will your own methods of handling conflict change as a result of completing this activity?

Extension:

Have the students role play some of the conflicts—first using the resolution/ending they observed, and then using a more effective strategy.

Conflict Observation Sheet

Directions: Observe one conflict every day for a week. As soon as you can after the conflict has ended, write down your answers to the following questions.

Monday

What was the conflict about? _____

_____

How many people were involved? _____

Describe what happened: _____

_____

Check all methods that were used to resolve or end the conflict:

   ___ fight or argument   ___ putting it off   ___ apologizing
   ___ sharing or taking turns   ___ humor   ___ compromise
   ___ asking for help   ___ problem solving or negotiation
   ___ other _____

Tuesday

What was the conflict about? _____

_____

How many people were involved? _____

Describe what happened: _____

_____

Check all methods that were used to resolve or end the conflict:

   ___ fight or argument   ___ putting it off   ___ apologizing
   ___ sharing or taking turns   ___ humor   ___ compromise
   ___ asking for help   ___ problem solving or negotiation
   ___ other _____

Wednesday
What was the conflict about?_____

_____

How many people were involved?_____

Describe what happened: _____

_____

Check all methods that were used to resolve or end the conflict:
___ fight or argument   ___ putting it off   ___ apologizing
___ sharing or taking turns   ___ humor   ___ compromise
___ asking for help   ___ problem solving or negotiation
___ other _____

Thursday
What was the conflict about?_____

_____

How many people were involved?_____

Describe what happened: _____

_____

Check all methods that were used to resolve or end the conflict:
___ fight or argument   ___ putting it off   ___ apologizing
___ sharing or taking turns   ___ humor   ___ compromise
___ asking for help   ___ problem solving or negotiation
___ other _____

Friday
What was the conflict about?_____

_____

How many people were involved?_____

Describe what happened: _____

_____

Check all methods that were used to resolve or end the conflict:
___ fight or argument   ___ putting it off   ___ apologizing
___ sharing or taking turns   ___ humor   ___ compromise
___ asking for help   ___ problem solving or negotiation
___ other _____

Experience Sheet

How Would You Handle This Conflict?

Writing, Sharing, and Discussion

Objectives:

The students will:
— describe in writing a personal conflict experience.
— identify and evaluate strategies for resolving conflicts.

Grades:

5-8

Materials:

writing materials for the students; chalkboard and chalk

Procedure:

Ask the students to think of conflict situations they have faced when it was hard to decide what to do. Discuss a few examples, including one from *your own* experience.

Explain the writing assignment: Ask the students to write about one personal conflict experience, without putting their names on their stories. Announce that the students will have 30 minutes to complete the writing. Students who finish writing their stories before time is up may write about a second conflict.

Collect the stories. Prepare for the second part of this activity by reading all of the stories to yourself and selecting four or five to review aloud. Try to select stories that:

- reflect typical conflicts that the students can relate to.
- provide enough detailed information to give the reader/listener most or all pertinent facts.

Begin the second session by reading one of the stories aloud. Emphasize that the identity of the student who wrote the story is not important.

Have the class brainstorm possible ways to manage/resolve the conflict described in the story. Write at least ten suggestions on the chalkboard. On a second chalkboard, list ideas that come up about conflict and conflict resolution in general.

Circle the suggestions that the students generally agree are best. If time allows, repeat the procedure with other stories you have selected. Conclude with a class discussion.

Discussion Questions:

1. What methods of responding to conflict are responsible? What methods are irresponsible? Why?
2. What kinds of things determine which conflict resolution strategy works best?
3. How can you control your feelings in a conflict situation?
4. What have you learned about conflict and conflict resolution from completing this activity?

Extension:

Have volunteers role play the best solutions (those that you circled) for each conflict.

Peer Mediation Practice 1
What a Conflict Manager Does

Objectives:

The students will:
— practice a seven-step peer mediation process.
— identify strengths and weaknesses within the process.

Grades:

3-8

Materials:

the steps in the peer mediation process, written on chart paper or the chalkboard

Procedure:

Tell the students that you are going to review the steps that Conflict Managers follow when they work with students to resolve a conflict. Ask three volunteers to come to the front of the room. (If you want your peer mediators to work in pairs, use four volunteers.) Ask one volunteer to play the role of the Conflict Manager. Ask the other two volunteers to play the roles of the disputants. Privately read them this situation:

Roger and Lita are arguing loudly in the hallway. Lita had promised to bring a book to school that she borrowed from Roger, but forgot. Roger is fed up, because this is the fourth day in a row that Lita has come to school without the book, which he needs to finish a report that's due tomorrow. Lita feels terrible about forgetting the book, but she also feels humiliated and defensive because Roger is making such a scene in the hallway. A small crowd has gathered.

Walk the Conflict Manager through the following steps, coaching him/her as you go. Encourage the other players in their roles, too.

1. Establish a Contract

Introduce yourself. Say, "Hi, my name is _____, and I'm a Conflict Manager.

Ask Roger and then Lita if they want your help in resolving the conflict. If they say yes, go to a neutral place where you will have privacy. Explain and get agreement to these rules:
- Do not interrupt the other person.
- Do not engage in name calling, put downs, or fighting.
- When it is your turn to speak, be as honest as you can.
- Agree to find a resolution to the conflict.
- Observe confidentiality. (Everything that happens here stays here.)

After you explain a rule, stop and ask the disputants individually if they agree to follow the rule. Do not proceed unless you have agreement on all of the rules. Decide who will speak first.

2. Define the Problem.

Ask Roger what happened and how he feels. Restate in your own words what you hear Roger say to make sure you understand. If you are unclear about anything, ask for more information:
— What do you mean by that?
— Tell me more about that.
— I don't understand. Can you give an example?

Summarize what you have heard, and then repeat the process with Lita.

3. Ask for Concessions.

Ask Lita what she can do to resolve the part(s) of the problem for which she is responsible. Ask Roger the same question. Encourage both disputants to think of things they as individuals can do to resolve the problem (*not* to make suggestions concerning what the other person can do).

4. Brainstorm Solutions.

Help the disputants think of possible solutions to the problem. List on paper as many solutions as they can think of. Do not allow them to criticize or evaluate the suggestions during the brainstorming process.

5. Evaluate Solutions.

Discuss each alternative with Roger and Lita. Help them decide which ones will work and which ones will not.

6. Choose a Solution.

Help Roger and Lita agree on a solution (or combination of solutions). Make sure neither is pressured into accepting a solution.

7. Get Agreement.

Ask Roger and Lita if the conflict is resolved. Remind them not to mention details of what took place to anyone. Congratulate them for their efforts.

Have groups of three students practice the steps, using the following situations. Instruct them to switch roles with each situation, one acting as the Conflict Manager, and the other two role playing the disputants in the conflict. (If your peer mediator's are working in pairs, use groups of four, with two Conflict Managers.)

Situations:

Larry tells several kids in class that he heard Ron's parents fighting and talking about a divorce when he was over at Ron's house on the weekend. Someone mentions it to Ron, who gets very upset. He confronts Larry and calls him a liar. They start to push each other around.

Rachel opens Sue's desk without asking and starts going through it, looking for an eraser she loaned Sue earlier. Sue comes up and demands to know what Rachel is doing. Rachel says, "None of your business." and starts to walk away. Sue shouts, "Give me what you took from my desk!" Rachel turns and says, "Make me!"

Bob is practicing footwork with a soccer ball on the field. Sarah asks if she can practice with him, but he says no. She tells him it's not fair for him to have the ball all recess, but he just ignores her. When he's not expecting it, Sarah kicks the ball away from him and takes off across the field. Bob runs after her and grabs the ball away. They start to fight.

Discussion Questions:

1. When you were the Conflict Manager, what did you find hardest? Why? What did you find easiest? Why?
2. Why is it important to have both disputants define the problem?
3. How can you be sure you are giving equal time to both disputants?
4. What can you do if one of the disputants tries to monopolize the time?
5. What can you do if a disputant keeps interrupting, or breaks some other rule?
6. Do you think it will be hard to remain neutral sometimes? What can you do about that?
7. What parts of this process do you need to work on most?

Peer Mediation Practice 2
Identifying the Problem

Objectives:

The students will:
— identify the problem of each disputant in a conflict situation.
— state that conflicts have different parts.
— use open-ended questions to help define a problem.

Grades:

3-8

Materials:

one copy of the experience sheet, "What Is the Problem?" for each student

---

Procedure:

Announce that in this activity, the students are going to focus on identifying the problem in conflict situations. Discuss the importance of understanding what the conflict is about before working on solutions.

Distribute the experience sheets and give the students a few minutes to complete them. Then ask the students to form groups of four to six and share what they have written. Have them discuss their answers and try to agree on two descriptions of the problem—the one that Liz would give and the one that Shawn would give.

Ask the groups to report their final problem descriptions to the class. Compare and discuss. Then say to the students, "Imagine that I am one of the disputants in a conflict, but I'm having trouble describing both the problem and my feelings. What kinds of questions can you ask me so that you can identify the problem correctly?"

As the students ask you questions, play the role. Respond the way you think you would if the situation were real. For example, when the questions are closed-ended, simply answer yes or no. When they are threatening, act defensive. When they are open-ended, provide more information. After your role play, discuss the benefits of asking open-ended questions like these:
— *How did you feel when it happened?*
— *How are you feeling right now?*
— *What didn't you like about what he did?*
— *Can you give an example of how she was unfair?*
— *Can you say more about that?*

If time permits, describe more conflict scenarios to the students and ask them the same questions that were on their experience sheet— this time orally. Conclude the activity with a discussion.

Discussion Questions:

1. Why is it important to identify the problem correctly?
2. When two disputants see the problem very differently, how can you get them to accept one another's views?
3. What can you do if a disputant refuses to talk? ...is too upset to talk?
4. What can you do if a disputant starts to cry?

What Is the Problem?

Read the story and answer the questions.

Liz is using the computer to write a story. She leaves for a few minutes to look up a word in the dictionary. While she is gone, Shawn sits down and starts reading her story. He starts to laugh at a funny part and accidentally leans on the keyboard. When Liz comes back, she discovers that part of her story is missing. She yells at Shawn, who denies doing anything. They start to argue.

1. What's the problem for Liz? _____

_____

2. How do you think she feels? _____

_____

3. What's the problem for Shawn?

_____

_____

4. How do you think he feels? _____

_____

5. What questions could you ask to find out if there are any more parts to the problem?

_____

_____

_____

_____

Peer Mediation Practice 3

Finding the Best Resolution

Objectives:

The students will:
— identify the parts of the problem for both disputants in conflict situations.
— describe resolutions that solve all parts of the problem.

Grades:

5-8

Materials:

one copy of the experience sheet, "The Parts Department" for each student; chalkboard and chalk

---

Procedure:

Begin by asking the students to think of the last time they were involved in a conflict. Ask them to recall the details of the conflict and how they resolved it. Ask volunteers to share their conflict and solution with the class. Note strategies and other significant points on the chalkboard.

Choose one example and question that student more closely. Ask if the problem could have been solved in two or three other ways. Specify the ways.

Choose another example—one in which the conflict seems to have several parts—and ask the students to help you break down the parts to the problem on the board. For example, if a student had a conflict with her sister because the sister borrowed a dress without asking and then returned it with a big stain on the front, the parts are:
— borrowing without permission
— the stained (and unwearable) dress

Point out that to find a good resolution to the conflict, both parts of the problem must be solved. In addition, the point of view of the sister must be considered and each of the parts of her problem identified. Write this sentence on the board:

In a good resolution, all parts of the problem from the point of view of both disputants are solved.

Distribute the experience sheets. Explain to the students that you want them to interview two people about a recent conflict they had with someone. Say: *Your job is to get enough information about both sides of the conflict to separate all the parts of the problem and come up with a good resolution. Since you will be talking to only one of the people who was involved in the conflict, you will have to do a little extra work to understand the other person's point of view.*

Have the students share the results of their completed experience sheets in groups of four to six. Instruct the groups to discuss each conflict in some depth to see if there are parts to the problem that have not been identified, to suggest more alternatives, and to change the resolution if they can agree on a better one. Since each group will be working on as many as twelve conflicts, you may want to split this task into two or three sessions.

Lead a follow-up discussion.

Discussion Questions:

1. What was the hardest part of this assignment? ...the easiest?
2. What kinds of questions did you ask when you were trying to discover all parts of a problem?
3. Does knowing all parts of a problem make finding a solution easier or harder? Explain.
4. How did this assignment change your ability to understand the other person's point of view in conflicts that you have?

The Parts Department

Interview two people about a conflict. Ask them to tell you what happened and what the problem was for them and for the other person in the conflict. Write down a description of the problem and then answer the questions.

Conflict #1
Describe the conflict. _____

_____

What are the parts of the problem for disputant #1? _____

_____

What are the parts of the problem for disputant #2? _____

_____

List all the alternatives for solving the problem that you can think of. _____

_____

_____

Go back and circle the alternative (or combination of alternatives) that you think will work best.

Conflict #2
Describe the conflict. _____

_____

What are the parts of the problem for disputant #1? _____

_____

What are the parts of the problem for disputant #2? _____

_____

List all the alternatives for solving the problem that you can think of. _____

_____

_____

Go back and circle the alternative (or combination of alternatives) that you think will work best.

Experience Sheet

Peer Mediation Practice 4
Solutions vs. Needs

Objectives:

The students will:
— distinguish between the needs of disputants in conflict situations and their initial solutions.
— describe ways of encouraging disputants to talk about their real needs.

Grades:

6-8

Materials:

one copy of the experience sheet, "Find the Hidden Need" for each student; chalkboard and chalk

Procedure:

Explain to the students that when working with disputants, it helps to be able to separate the disputant's initial solution statements from the disputant's real needs. Lots of times, people already have a problem solved in their own minds, so all they want to talk about is their solution. Sometimes they don't even mention the need which that solution is supposed to satisfy. List these examples on the board:

Solution Statements

"Keep your shoes off the couch."
"Don't ever touch my clothes again!"
"You have to give me a ride Saturday morning."
"Stop all that talking and laughing."

Need Statements

"I need to have a clean couch."
"I need my clothes to be here and in good shape when I want to wear them."
"I need to be at practice on time Saturday morning."
"I need quiet so I can concentrate."

Ask the students to think of some additional examples from their own experience. Have them challenge each other to figure out the needs behind their solution statements.

Distribute the experience sheets and give the students a few minutes to fill them out. Then have the students form groups of four to six and go through the solution statements one at a time. After each statement is read, have members take turns explaining what they think the needs behind the solution statement are. Tell the groups to come to consensus concerning the needs in all five examples. Have the groups report to the class. Lead a follow-up discussion.

Discussion Questions:

1. Why is it easier to talk about our solution to a problem than it is to talk about what we really need?
2. What kinds of questions can you ask to encourage a disputant to express his or her real needs?
3. Sometimes when disputants hear each other's real needs, the conflict cools down almost immediately. Why do you think that is?
4. What have you learned from this activity that will help you manage your own conflicts?

Find the Hidden Need

Read each statement. Then write down the needs behind the statement. There may be more than one need. Example:

Solution statement:
"This is the third time I've missed the bus waiting for you. You're not my friend anymore."

Needs:
    I need to catch my bus.
    I need to be able to count on my friends.

Solution statement:
"Stop criticizing me all the time. If you think I'm so stupid, find another partner."

Needs: _____

_____

_____

Solution statement:
"I thought just you and I were going to the movie. If she goes, I'm not going."

Needs: _____

_____

_____

Experience Sheet

Solution statement: ➡️

"I told you about that problem at least three times. I'm going to quit telling you things."

Needs: _____

_____

_____

_____

Solution statement:

"I had this tennis court reserved. You'll have to find another one."

Needs: _____

_____

_____

_____

Solution statement: ➡️

"No, I won't loan you my calculator. The last time I loaned you something, you broke it."

Needs: _____

_____

_____

_____

A Time We Needed Help to Resolve a Conflict

A Sharing Circle

Objectives:

The students will:
— describe a conflict in which the help of a third party was needed.
— identify helpful behaviors on the part of a conflict mediator.

Grades:

K-8

Introduce the Topic:

Our topic for this session is, "A Time We Needed Help to Resolve a Conflict." All of us get into conflicts with our family and friends. Much of the time, we work things out without getting anyone else involved. But sometimes a conflict is too big or too upsetting to handle without help. Can you remember such a time? Maybe you and a brother or sister were arguing over whose turn it was to mow the lawn, and you had to ask one of your parents to help figure it out. Or maybe you had a conflict with a friend over something you were told he or she said about you behind your back, and it took the help of another friend to get the two of you back together. Perhaps you and a classmate had to ask the teacher to settle an argument over who had the correct answer to a problem, or maybe you had to let your coach help settle a fight between you and a teammate. Think about it for a few moments, and tell us what the conflict was about and what the third person did to help you settle it. The topic is, "A Time We Needed Help to Resolve a Conflict."

Discussion Questions:

1. What were some of the reasons that we had to ask for help?
2. When is it a good idea to let someone else help you resolve a conflict?
3. If you ask for help resolving a conflict and the person you ask just comes over and tells you what to do, is that helpful? Why or why not?
4. What kind of help *is* helpful in resolving a conflict?

When One Person Kept Blaming Another for Causing a Problem

A Sharing Circle

Objectives:

The students will:
— a time when blaming perpetuated a conflict.
— state why blaming is counterproductive to conflict resolution.

Grades:

K-8

Introduce the Topic:

Today in our Sharing Circle, we're going to talk about times when we were part of the "blame game." Our topic is, "When One Person Kept Blaming Another for Causing a Problem."

Blaming is something we are all tempted to do at times. But it usually isn't very helpful. Saying a problem is someone else's fault may get us out of trouble, but it usually doesn't solve the problem. Can you think of a time when you saw one person blame another for just about every part of a problem? Maybe you know someone who gets in trouble a lot and always says it's someone else's fault. Or maybe you have a brother or sister who blames you for just about every problem that comes up at home. Have you heard government leaders who always seem to be blaming each other instead of taking responsibility? Have you tried to settle fights between younger children in which it was hard to figure out what happened because each child blamed the other? Think about it for a few moments. Tell us what happened and how you felt, but don't use any names. The topic is, "When One Person Kept Blaming Another for Causing a Problem."

Discussion Questions:

1. Why is blaming not a helpful thing to do?
2. How do you feel when someone blames you for something?
3. If you're trying to help two people settle a conflict, how can you get them to stop blaming each other?

Additional Sharing Circle Topics

A Time When Sharing Prevented a Fight

I Solved a Problem Effectively

A Time I Was Afraid to Face a Conflict

I Tried to Solve a Problem Too Soon

A Time Humor Saved the Day

I Faced a Problem on My Own

We Compromised to Get It Done

When the Easy Way Out Made Things Worse

How I Helped a Friend Resolve a Conflict

Putting It All Together

Students spend a good portion of their time at school, but their young lives have larger arenas too, and so do their spheres of influence.

The purpose of this section is to give you and your students opportunities to find broader application for the tools and strategies of conflict resolution, by examining issues, problems, and conflicts in the community, nation, and world.

It's fairly safe to assume that students who internalize effective conflict resolution strategies through experiences in the classroom and school will take those same behaviors with them into the community. They will also be capable of using them as citizens to influence national and international issues and conflicts. But why just assume? Even very young students can begin to apply concepts they are learning in their own lives to the world around them. They can recognize conflict in the community, nation, and the world, they can generate workable solutions, and they can take steps to see that those solutions are implemented.

The activities in this section are designed to help students:

- Develop a classroom bill of rights.
- Discuss the value of peace and identify how their actions contribute to peace on a wider scale.
- Recognize differences in styles of authority and learn methods of effectively responding to authority figures.
- Apply problem-solving methods to school and community problems.
- Through the use of current-events articles, apply problem-solving methods to world issues.
- Develop resolutions to conflicts in the news.
- Identify ways they can contribute to the community.
- Identify ways they can contribute to global peace.

Protect Your Rights!
Developing a Classroom Bill of Rights

Objectives:

The students will:
— explain how knowing one another's rights prevents conflict.
— develop and vote on a *Classroom Bill of Rights*.

Grades:

K-8

Materials:

a display copy of the *U.S. Bill of Rights*; writing materials for the students

Procedure:

Note: This activity is written for students who read and write. Very young students will need to develop their list of rights orally, as a class. Record their contributions on the chalkboard, and transfer the final list to chart paper.

Begin with a class discussion on the U.S. Constitution's *Bill of Rights*. Display a list of the rights, and talk about each one. Point out that one of the reasons our country has a *Bill of Rights* is to help prevent conflicts between individuals and between individual citizens and the government.

Announce that the students are going to draw up a *Classroom Bill of Rights* to help prevent conflicts between students, and between individual students and yourself.

Brainstorm a list of areas in which written rights might be appropriate and helpful. Write suggested items on the chalkboard. For example, the students might want to develop written rights in the following areas:
• expression of feelings
• expression of beliefs and opinions

• giving and receiving respect
• respect of property (e.g., desk and contents)
• work and study
• quiet and privacy
• help and assistance
• violence and peer pressure
• fair hearing in conflict situations

Have the students form committees of four to six. Divide the categories among the committees, and ask the committees to develop written rights for each of their areas. Suggest that they start by selecting a chairperson and secretary.

Have the chairpersons form a special delegation whose job it is to combine the lists, eliminate duplications, make necessary changes, and then submit a final draft to the class for approval. Examine and discuss each proposed right with the students and vote to approve, disapprove, or recommend that it receive further study and work. Return items requiring further work to their original committees. If a suggested right is at odds with school policy, explain the problem and return it to committee.

Have volunteers record the final *Classroom Bill of Rights* on chart paper for display in the classroom.

Discussion Questions:

1. What are "rights" and how do we get them?
2. Which of the rights we've developed are most important to you and why?
3. How will having a *Classroom Bill of Rights* help prevent conflict? How will it help resolve conflict?
4. If someone in the class violates one of your rights, what can you do about it?

Extension:

Involve the entire school in the project. Have classes appoint a representative to each of the established committees. Hold a constitutional convention to finalize and ratify the *School Bill of Rights*.

Promoting Peace

A Brainstorming Activity

Objectives:

The students will:
— learn and practice a brainstorming process.
— name specific ways individuals can demonstrate the value of peace.
— describe significant contributions to world peace and state who made them.

Grades:

2-8

Materials:

chalkboard and chalk; stopwatch or watch with secondhand

Procedure:

Begin with a discussion about peace. Point out that peace is the opposite of conflict. This is true for internal as well as external conflict. When an individual is free of internal conflict she or he feels peaceful inside. Two friends have peace in their relationship when they are not arguing or fighting. Groups, nations, and the world are at peace when they are free of conflict. Ask the students if they value peace. Most will say yes. Then write this assignment on the board:

— Name all the ways you can think of for us to communicate our value of peace to others.
— Name as many people as you can think of who have contributed to world peace in a significant way and describe how they did it.

Announce that the class as a whole is going to brainstorm these two lists. Get agreement on the following rules for brainstorming:

Rules for Brainstorming

1. Think of as many possible suggestions as you can in the allotted time.
2. Use your imagination and be creative.
3. Do not question, criticize, or evaluate any suggestion during the brainstorming process.
4. After the brainstorming period is closed, go back and evaluate/discuss the suggestions.
5. Through consensus, agree on a final list.

Announce that the students will have 3 minutes to brainstorm each list. Appoint a timekeeper and begin brainstorming the first list. Record suggested items on the board. At the end of 3 minutes, brainstorm the second list. When time is up, go back and discuss the items on the first list, achieving consensus on a final list. Do the same with the second list. Suggest that the students judge the items on the first list based on how specific and realistic they are (whether or not they are doable) and on whether or not they will achieve the goal (communicating the value of peace). Evaluate of the second list based on the suggested person's deeds and the impact of those deeds on the world.

Permanently display the final lists on a bulletin board. Complete the activity with a class discussion.

Discussion Questions:

1. Why is it important to know how to communicate the things we value to others?
2. If we don't communicate the values we have, how will others know we have them?
3. When you promote peace as an individual, how are you contributing to world peace?
4. Can valuing peace make us better conflict managers? How?

Three Kinds of Authority
Creative Dramatics and Discussion

Objectives:

The students will:
— demonstrate an understanding of different styles of authority.
— practice responding to different styles of authority in ways that effectively avoid or resolve conflict.
— identify individual patterns of reacting to authority figures.

Grades:

2-8

Materials:

a few props for the dramatizations (optional)

Procedure:

Introduce the activity by engaging the students in a discussion about authority and authority figures. Suggest that people in positions of authority (law enforcement officers, teachers, parents, supervisors, coaches, etc.) deal with their subordinates in many ways, most of which can be classified according to three styles: *dominant, cooperative,* and *indifferent.* Elaborate with one or two examples. For instance, you could say:

Imagine a teacher taking a group of students on a field trip. A dominant teacher might post a list of rules in advance, order the students to follow them, and threaten students who didn't with detention or a parent conference. A cooperative teacher might ask the students to help develop a list of rules for the trip, specifying the consequences for breaking each rule. An indifferent teacher might fail to mention behavior at all, and then either make light of problems that arise or ignore them altogether.

Point out that all kids sometimes have conflicts with authority figures. Understanding these styles can help students respond appropriately.

Generate some discussion of appropriate responses by asking these questions:
— *If a police officer orders a person out of his or her car, would it make sense for the person to suggest an alternative like inviting the officer to get into the car instead?*
— *If your parent says, "How shall we handle this?", what is he or she asking for?*
— *If you ask a teacher for help and she or he says, "Don't bother me now," what can you do?*

Tell the students that you'd like them to role play some scenarios involving authority. Explain:

Each scenario will be dramatized three times, with a different student playing the part of the authority figure each time. The first student will play the part using a dominant style, the second student will use a cooperative style, and the third an indifferent style. The other actors in the scenario will remain in their roles throughout all three versions, adjusting their reactions to fit the style of authority being used.

Set up each scenario with simple props (optional) and choose volunteers to play the parts. Allow a minute or two of action before switching from one style of authority to another.

Situations:

1. Students are in a classroom studying, when a strong wind comes up outside and begins blowing violently through the windows, which are covered with open horizontal blinds. The blinds are banging and papers are flying. The teacher is the only one in the room who knows how to shut the windows; however, the blinds are very heavy, andhe or she needs help lifting them up in order to get to the windows. Play the teacher as dominant, cooperative, and indifferent.

2. Five students are working on a project together. They are trying to agree on how to write their report and their discussion is getting fairly loud and disruptive. Other students in the class have stopped their work and are watching and making comments. The teacher gets up from his or her desk and heads for the group. Play the teacher as dominant, cooperative, and indifferent.

3. A student has collapsed on the field. Several other students have gathered around, and there is a lot of shouting and confusion. Someone calls a teacher, who runs over. Play the teacher as dominant, cooperative, and indifferent.

4. A group of students arrives at a gas station very early on Saturday morning to hold a car wash. The students have permission to use the station lot, but there has not been any prior communication with the station owner about what they can and can't do. The students are already connecting up their hoses and putting up balloons and posters when the station owner arrives. Play the owner as dominant, cooperative, and indifferent.

5. At the urging of her parent, a girl who is frequently teased and tormented by other students goes to see the school principal for help and advice. Play the principal as dominant, cooperative, and indifferent.

After *each* scenario has been enacted in all three ways, lead a brief discussion. Ask these questions:
— *How did you feel when you were dealing with the dominant style of authority? ...the cooperative style? ...the indifferent style?*
— *How did your responses differ among the three styles?*
— *How did changing your own style help you avoid a conflict?*
— *Which style was easiest for you to respond to? Why?*
— *Which style is hardest for you to respond to? Why?*

After all of the scenarios have been enacted, lead a culminating discussion.

Discussion Questions:

1. Why is it a good idea for you to change your way of responding to fit the style of authority?
2. With which style of authority is it best to avoid conflict? Why?
3. With which style of authority is conflict most apt to result in a positive outcome? Why?
4. What have you learned from this activity?

Community Action!

Brainstorming, Planning, and Discussion

Objectives:

The students will:
— choose a school or community problem to work on as a class.
— brainstorm solutions to the problem.
— choose a solution and develop a plan of action.

Grades:

2-8

Materials:

one piece of chart paper and a magic marker for each group; chalkboard and chalk

Procedure:

Note: If you teach students in grades two through four, focus on a school problem. If you teach students in grades five through eight, consider focusing on a community problem. If your students are non readers/writers, conduct the activity with the entire class, illustrating suggestions with symbols and key words on the board or chart paper.

Announce that the class is going to work on solving a school/community problem. Begin by brainstorming specific problems that you and the students are aware of. (See rules for brainstorming, page 170.) For example, a school problem might be lack of funds for repainting. A community problem might be the need for safer neighborhoods. Write all suggestions on the board.

Evaluate the suggestions and choose one, preferably through consensus.

Have the students form groups of five to eight. Ask them to select a leader and a recorder. Distribute the chart paper and markers.

Again, remind the students of the rules for brainstorming. Tell them to brainstorm as many solutions to the problem as they can in 10 minutes. Call time, and instruct the groups to go back and discuss/evaluate each of their suggestions. Tell them to ask themselves these questions:
— *Can we really do this?*
— *Will this solution solve (or help solve) the problem?*
— *Would this solution work better if it were combined with another solution?*

After eliminating unworkable suggestions, have the groups select one solution to recommend to the class. If the groups experience conflict during any part of this process, guide them to use conflict resolution strategies that they have learned.

Display and evaluate the solutions of the various groups, answering the questions listed above for each one. Using consensus, select one solution to implement. (Your job is to influence the students to keep their solution simple and workable.)

In a second session, conduct a planning meeting. Break down the solution into specific steps and tasks, identifying needed resources. Develop a timeline. Appoint teams of volunteers to be responsible for each step/task.

Following implementation of the solution, discuss and evaluate the results.

Discussion Questions:

1. To what extent did we solve or help solve the problem?
2. Would another solution have worked better? If so, which one?
3. What problems or conflicts did you experience while completing your step or task?
4. How did you resolve those problems/conflicts?
5. Why is it important to be a good conflict manager when working with others on a project?

Kids Can Solve Problems

Current Events Research, Brainstorming, and Discussion

Objectives:

The students will:
— select and summarize a current-events article dealing with an important issue or event.
— generate solutions to a current-events problem presented by the teacher.
— in small groups, achieve consensus on a solution to the problem.

Grades:

2-8

Materials:

current-events articles (brought by the students from home); an article to read to the students; the "rules for brainstorming" displayed on chart paper or chalkboard (page 170)

Preparation:

Ask the students to cut a current-events article from a newspaper or news magazine and bring it to school on the day of the activity. Require that the articles deal with an issue or event of some importance. Bring an article of your own dealing with a problem for which creative solutions are obviously needed.

Procedure:

Talk to the students about the importance of being well-informed. Explain that the community, the nation, and the world are made up of individuals such as they. The world is shaped by the interest and participation of individual people working together. People build, produce, feed, govern, and educate. In the process, they create conflicts and problems, which they also must solve. Ask the students what kinds of issues, events, and problems they discovered while reading the newspaper. Ask two or three volunteers to briefly tell the class about their articles.

Have the students share their article with a partner. Allow about 5 minutes for this. Then read *your* article aloud to the class. Define terms used in the article, and discuss the problem. Ask these questions:
— *What is the problem?*
— *Whose problem is it?*

Announce that through group discussion, the students are going to come up with solutions to the problem described in the article. Have the students form groups of three to five. Give them 1 minute to choose a leader and a recorder. Then announce that the groups will have 10 minutes to brainstorm solutions to the problem. Direct their attention to the posted rules of brainstorming and review, as necessary.

Call time after 10 minutes, and have the groups discuss and evaluate their suggestions, one at a time. Their task is to choose one solution to present to the class. Suggest that they answer these questions:
— *Will this solution solve the problem?*
— *Can this solution actually be done?*
— *Will combining any suggestions make a better solution?*

Allow a few more minutes for discussion. Urge the groups to use the process of consensus-seeking to make their decision. Have the group leaders report the class. Then lead a culminating discussion.

Discussion Questions:

1. What was the hardest part about finding a solution to this problem? What was the easiest part?
2. If your group was not able to come to a decision, why not?
3. How were disagreements or conflicts handled in your group?
4. Is there any way for individuals or nations to avoid having problems? Explain.
5. How will learning to solve problems here in the classroom help prepare us to solve them in the outside world?

It's a Small World

Group Consensus-Seeking on World Issues

Objectives:

The students will:
— summarize a news article about a world issue/problem.
— define the main issue/problem addressed in the article.
— brainstorm solutions to selected issues/problems in small groups.
— use consensus to decide on courses of action.

Grades:

4-8

Materials:

one copy of the experience sheet, "World Issues" for each student; student-selected articles cut from newspapers and news magazines; chart paper and markers; the "rules of brainstorming" displayed on chart paper or chalkboard (page 170)

Preparation:

A day or two prior to leading this activity, distribute and go over the experience sheets, asking the students to complete them as homework. Remind them that the articles they choose must be about world problems.

Procedure:

Ask the students to help you define the term *issue*. Write their suggestions on the board and interject some of your own. Consider these dictionary components:
—*an unsettled matter needing a decision*
—*a matter of disagreement between two or more parties*
—*a point of debate or controversy*

Ask the students to take out their homework. Ask them how well their definition of *issue* fits the news articles they chose. Discuss briefly, and then announce that the students are going to work in small groups to develop solutions to one issue per group.

Have students form groups of four to six and choose a leader and recorder. Distribute the chart paper and markers. Ask the students to take turns summarizing their articles. Suggest that they refer to their experience sheet, naming countries involved, explaining the issue, and summarizing what has been done about the issue so far. Allow about 5 minutes for this task.

Direct the groups to choose one issue on which to focus. Allow about 2 minutes for discussion and decision making. Ask the recorders to write a statement of the issue at the top of the chart paper. Then announce that the groups have 5 minutes to brainstorm alternative decisions or solutions to the selected issue. Remind them to follow the posted rules for brainstorming. After you call time, announce that the groups have 10 minutes to evaluate the suggested alternatives. Instruct them to cross out unworkable ideas and narrow their list down to the two or three best suggestions.

Have the recorders tape their lists to a wall in front of the class. Have the leaders take turns reporting their group's issue and possible decisions/solutions to the class. Ask the class to join in making a final decision concerning each issue. Lead a follow-up discussion.

Discussion Questions:

1. What was the hardest part about making a decision regarding your issue? What was the easiest part?
2. If your group was not able to come to a decision, why not?
3. How were disagreements or conflicts handled in your group?
4. What is the difference between an issue and a conflict?
5. How does conflict interfere with the ability of nations to decide what to do about world issues?
6. How do nations and world bodies like the U.N. resolve conflicts?
7. What have you learned from this activity that will enable you to help solve global problems?

Extension:

If time allows, have the students return to their groups and develop plans of action for implementing their solutions.

World Issues

Choose a recent article from a newspaper or news magazine. The article must be about a world issue or problem. For example, the article might deal with the global environment, world hunger, trading between nations, or world peace.

Read the article and answer these questions:

1. What is the issue or problem described in the article?_____

_____

_____

_____

_____

_____

_____

_____

2. What countries are involved? _____

_____

_____

_____

_____

3. What has been done about the issue or problem up to now? _____

_____

_____

_____

_____

_____

4. What suggestions, if any, does the writer make? _____

_____

_____

_____

_____

_____

5. List your own ideas for settling the issue. _____

_____

_____

_____

_____

_____

_____

Experience Sheet

Conflict in the News

Class Brainstorming and Consensus Seeking

Objectives:

The students will:
— review conflict resolution strategies.
— summarize a conflict taken from a news article.
— brainstorm alternative resolutions to a selected conflict.
— develop and describe a final resolution to the conflict.

Grades:

2-8

Materials:

news articles brought by the students from home; chart paper and markers or chalkboard and chalk

Preparation:

A day or two before you plan to implement this activity, ask the students to cut out and bring a news article dealing with any form of conflict—interpersonal, intergroup, or between nations.

Procedure:

Ask the students to sit in one large circle. Begin with a discussion about conflict. Remind the students of some of the things they have learned about conflict—that it is normal and unavoidable, that the causes of conflict can usually be described, and that they have learned a number of strategies for resolving conflict. Briefly review those strategies, listing them on chart paper or the chalkboard.

Go around the circle and ask each student to summarize in a few sentences his or her news article. After each summary, ask the group:
—*What is the conflict?*
—*Who is having the conflict?*

Ask the students to choose one article to focus on more closely. Explain that it should involve a conflict for which they as a group can

develop a workable solution. Lead the students through a process of discussion and consensus-seeking until a decision is reached.

Ask a volunteer (or aide) to be the group's recorder. Then lead the group in a 10-minute brainstorming session to generate possible resolutions to the conflict. Have the recorder write every suggestion on the board or chart paper. Don't allow evaluation of any kind during brainstorming.

Facilitate an evaluation of the alternatives listed. Eliminate duplications and suggestions that are obviously unrealistic. (Be careful not to eliminate suggestions just because they require new, creative approaches. These may be the best suggestions of all.) After you have narrowed the list, point to one remaining alternative at a time and ask the group:
—*What will happen to the people (groups, countries) involved if we choose this alternative?*
—*What are the chances that this alternative will resolve the conflict?*
—*What must each person (group, country) do in order to make this alternative work?*

—Would this alternative work better if we combined with it another one? Which one?

Help the students arrive at a consensus regarding the best resolution to the conflict. Conclude the activity with a discussion.

Discussion Questions:

1. What are some similarities and differences between interpersonal, intergroup, and international conflict?
2. Which of the strategies we've learned would work well in resolving conflicts between groups? ...between nations?

3. If you think you have a solution to a conflict you read about in the news, who can you tell about it and how?
4. Why is it important that each of us express our opinion and try to make a difference in the world?

Extension:

Ask two or three volunteers to collaborate on a "letter to the editor" of the newspaper or news magazine from which the article was taken. Have them describe the process the class used as well as the resolution chosen. Mail the letter. Display a copy of the letter in the classroom.

Something I've Done (or Could Do) to Improve Our Community

A Sharing Circle

Objectives:

The students will:
— describe ways in which they can contribute to the betterment of the community.
— explain how community involvement can help to prevent and resolve conflict.

Grades:

K-8

Introduce the Topic:

The topic for the session is, "Something I've Done (or Could Do) to Improve Our Community." Can you think of a time when you did something that you felt really helped, even in a small way, to improve the community we live in? Perhaps you improved the condition of your neighborhood by cleaning up yards, empty lots, and streets. Or perhaps you did something to help our environment—like try to use less water and electricity. Maybe you helped in an effort to find homes for stray animals or shelter for homeless people. Whatever it was, we would like to hear about it. If you can't think of something you've already done, perhaps you can think of something you would like to do in the future, *either independently or with a group. Our topic is, "Something I've Done (or Could Do) to Improve Our Community."*

Discussion Questions:

1. How do you feel when you do something that helps improve our community?
2. How can we encourage more people to get involved in improving our community?
3. How can working together to improve our community help prevent and resolve conflict between individuals and groups?

Something I Can Do to Promote Peace in the World

A Sharing Circle

Objectives:

The students will:
— identify ways in which they can contribute to world peace.
— name recent world events that have promoted global peace.

Grades:

K-8

Introduce the Topic:

We've been talking a lot about conflict between people, and how, when we are free of conflict, we feel peaceful inside. Today in our circle, we're going to talk about peace on a much broader scale. We're going to talk about global peace. Our topic is, "Something I Can Do to Promote Peace in the World."

What can you do as a student and a citizen to make the world a more peaceful place? Maybe you can join an organization that works for peace, or write letters to members of congress asking them to do more to promote peace in the world. Perhaps you can send food to people in other parts of the world who are being hurt by war. Reading the newspaper so that you know what is going on in the world is a good place to start. Keeping peace at home, at school, and in your neighborhood contributes to world peace,

too. Does your church or synagogue have activities that promote peace? Have you ever written a letter to a member of the armed services who can't come home for the holidays? Think about it for a few moments and tell us about a way that you can make a difference. The topic is, "Something I Can Do to Promote Peace in the World."

Discussion Questions:

1. How do you feel when you do something that helps others?
2. Why is it important to help people in other parts of the world?
3. Some very important things have happened in the last few years that have given us more peace in the world. What are they?
4. How can we ensure that peace in the world keeps growing?

Additional Sharing Circle Topics

A Problem in My Neighborhood That Needs To Be Solved

A Situation in Which I Behaved Responsibly

I Helped Someone Who Needed and Wanted My Help

A World Problem That I'd Like to Help Solve

I Didn't Do Something Because I Knew It Would Hurt Someone

Something I Do to Protect the Environment

When a Stranger Needed Some Help

Something I've Done or Could Do to Improve Our World